Romantic Weddings

25 Handcrafted Accessories and Keepsakes

Rebekah Meier

NORTH LIGHT BOOKS
Cincinnati, Ohio
www.artistsnetwork.com

10 09 08 07 06   5 4 3 2 1

Distributed in Canada by Fraser Direct
100 Armstrong Avenue
Georgetown, ON, Canada L7G 5S4
Tel: (905) 877-4411

Distributed in the U.K. and Europe
by David & Charles
Brunel House, Newton Abbot, Devon,
TQ12 4PU, England
Tel: (+44) 1626 323200, Fax: (+44) 1626 323319
Email: mail@davidandcharles.co.uk

Distributed in Australia by Capricorn Link
P.O. Box 704, S. Windsor, NSW 2756 Australia
Tel: (02) 4577-3555

EDITOR: JENNIFER FELLINGER

COVER DESIGNER: STEPHANIE STRANG

DESIGNER: MARISSA BOWERS

LAYOUT ARTIST: KATHY GARDNER

PRODUCTION COORDINATOR: JENNIFER WAGNER

PHOTOGRAPHERS: CHRISTINE POLOMSKY,
TIM GRONDIN, AL PARRISH, AND HAL BARKAN

PHOTO STYLIST: JANET A. NICKUM

F+W PUBLICATIONS, INC.

METRIC CONVERSION CHART

TO CONVERT	TO	MULTIPLY BY
Inches	Centimeters	2.54
Centimeters	Inches	0.4
Feet	Centimeters	30.5
Centimeters	Feet	0.03
Yards	Meters	0.9
Meters	Yards	1.1
Sq. Inches	Sq. Centimeters	6.45
Sq. Centimeters	Sq. Inches	0.16
Sq. Feet	Sq. Meters	0.09
Sq. Meters	Sq. Feet	10.8
Sq. Yards	Sq. Meters	0.8
Sq. Meters	Sq. Yards	1.2
Pounds	Kilograms	0.45
Kilograms	Pounds	2.2
Ounces	Grams	28.3
Grams	Ounces	0.035

Library of Congress Cataloging-in-Publication Data
Meier, Rebekah.
  Romantic weddings : 25 handcrafted accessories and keepsakes / Rebekah Meier.-- 1st ed.
      p. cm.
  Includes index.
  ISBN 1-55870-718-2 (alk. paper)
  1. Handicraft. 2. Wedding decorations. I. Title.
TT149.M45 2006
745.594'1--dc22

ABOUT THE AUTHOR

Rebekah Meier lives with her husband, Brad, and two sons, Dan and Matt, in northern Illinois, where she fulfills her lifelong passion for creating. A member of the Society of Craft Designers, Rebekah regularly teaches crafting classes. She has been published in several craft magazines and is a regular contributor to *Create & Decorate* magazine. Look for her next North Light book, *Sew Easy Papercrafting*, in 2006.

DEDICATION

I dedicate this book to my mother, Helen Kauffman. I could not have gotten this far without your daily help, wisdom and love. And to my loving husband, Brad, and sons, Dan and Matt—thank you for not expecting full-course dinners and dust-free tables.

ACKNOWLEDGMENTS

To everyone at North Light—your good hearts and professionalism have made my first book so rewarding. Thanks to Tricia Waddell, who asked me to write this book. Special thanks to Jenny Fellinger and Christine Polomsky, who took such good care of me, put me at ease and made me "feel" like an author!

Table of Contents

Introduction

What bride doesn't wish for the perfect romantic wedding? And what bride doesn't hope for a stress-free and worry-free wedding, in which everything comes together beautifully to create a memorable celebration?

As a bride-to-be, you may be wondering how you're going to pull it off. How will you make everything perfect without a premarriage meltdown? How will you make your wedding unique without succumbing to stress? And how will you get everything done before the big day without reaching the bridal boiling point? If you are asking these questions, you've come to the right place!

Let's face it—in today's world, "quick" and "easy" are the key to a less stressful, more enjoyable wedding. With simple step-by-step projects, *Romantic Weddings* shows you how to create special accessories and keepsakes that will serve as lasting reminders of your day. In the pages that follow, you'll find projects for every aspect of your wedding, from invitations to reception favors to honeymoon albums. And the best part is that all of the projects are quick and easy—most can be made in a single afternoon or evening.

I've designed each project with the guiding principle that everything should be simply romantic—evocative of romance without being overly complicated. Because the projects are simple, they are also adaptable; this means, rather than just imitating what you see on these pages, you can take the projects and make them your own. I encourage you to explore your personal style by experimenting with different colors and trying new types of papers and embellishments. In today's dynamic crafting marketplace, there is no shortage of beautiful wedding-related materials, so your options are endless!

As you plan your wedding details with friends and family, I hope you will let *Romantic Weddings* inspire your creative side. And while you're at it, why not share your inspiration with those around you? You might consider hosting a wedding craft party, where bridesmaids, close friends and family members can help make the projects. Add a little music and some food and drink, and you'll have a memorable night of crafting festivities. Your party guests will have fun— and they might even walk away with a case of crafting fever themselves. You'll have a whole set of wedding projects completed, ready to be checked off your to-do list. What a way to prepare for the wedding!

So, forget about stress, think romance and let this book inspire you to create the wedding of your dreams!

Materials

Most materials used for the projects in this book are readily available for purchase at your local fabric, craft and scrapbook stores, or online.

BEFORE BUYING YOUR MATERIALS

Going to the craft store and purchasing materials is always fun, but it can be a little overwhelming, especially if you haven't made one important decision first—what your color scheme will be.

Don't feel limited by the traditional wedding palette of white or ivory. For several projects, I've chosen soft colors, like tan, pink and light blue, to evoke a vintage romantic feeling. You, however, can select whichever colors strike your fancy. You might go with the colors of your bridesmaids' gowns or the flowers in your bouquet. The sky's the limit!

Once you have chosen the colors for your wedding, the fun really begins. I'm sure you have spent time searching for a wedding dress, veil, shoes and jewelry that reflect your personal style. Now it's time to explore the shops for paper, fabric and trimmings; these crafting accessories, like your wedding day attire, should represent your style. When used to create wedding craft projects, scrapbook embellishments, buttons, ribbon, lace and beads will all set the mood for your wedding.

With such a wide variety of beautiful products available to crafters today, the sky's the limit when choosing materials for your romantic-themed projects!

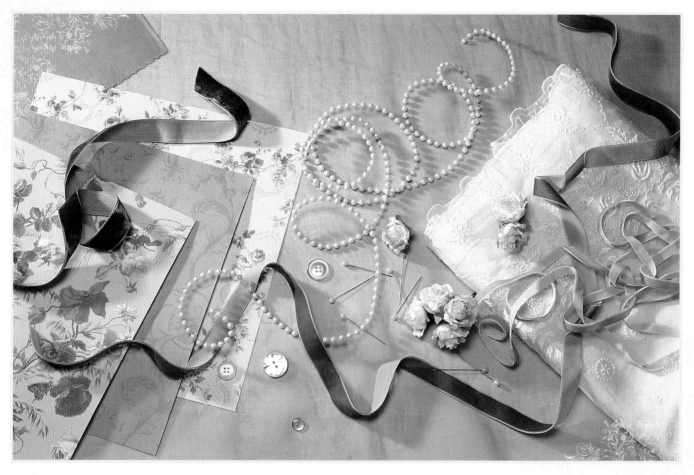

Explore your options for project surfaces and embellishments. Gorgeous surfaces, such as decorative paper and fabric, and exciting embellishments, such as ribbons, buttons, pearls, beads and fabric flowers, are readily available at fabric and craft supply stores.

SURFACES

Crafters use a wide variety of surfaces, including paper, fabric, wood and papier-mâché. For the most part, the projects in this book require a surface of paper or fabric. No matter what your surface, it is important to always purchase the best possible quality. If you're going to put work into handcrafting a keepsake—especially a keepsake for one of the most important days of your life—you want it to last for generations. A high-quality product ensures longevity.

Decorative Papers

These days, paper companies offer a fantastic array of colors, designs and patterns. To complement their paper products, many companies also sell coordinating trims, embellishments and stickers. Sometimes there are so many choices, it makes your head spin! But it can be great fun

to create a wedding design theme by mixing and matching decorative paper. If you are planning on using the same paper to create your own "line" of wedding stationery—invitations, programs, favors, thank-you notes and so on—you might consider purchasing the paper in large quantities. It pays to think ahead, as some paper stores will give you a discount if you spend or order a certain amount.

EMBELLISHMENTS

Check out your local craft store to brainstorm for embellishment ideas—you will be amazed by the selection. One of the great things about ribbons, pearls, beads and fabric flowers is that they can be dyed to match any color. So, do not fret if you find beautiful lace that is the "wrong" color. Simply dye it, and you will have the perfect lace right at your fingertips! Swarovski crystal beads are used as embellishments throughout the projects. I suggest not substituting regular beads for these crystals, as they add a uniquely elegant shimmer that is beyond compare.

PAINT

Several projects in this book call for acrylic paints and finishing sprays. Acrylics are a great option for everyone from the the novice crafter to the seasoned expert. Inexpensive and readily available in every craft store, acrylic paints come in a wide variety of colors. You're almost certain to find hues that match your chosen color scheme. Acrylic paints are easy to apply with a brush, and they clean up with water.

TIP IT IS ALWAYS IMPERATIVE to use the correct glue for the material(s) you are adhering. As you will see, I use everything from laminating liquid to hot glue; it all depends on the particular project. When gluing paper, use glue that is specifically designed for paper; the same goes for fabric, wood, jewelry and so on. For each project, I specify which adhesive is appropriate.

MISCELLANEOUS

When I work on craft projects, I experiment with all kinds of miscellaneous materials. I encourage you to do the same—you never know when you will come up with just the thing to solve a crafting dilemma or give your project a finishing touch.

There are several miscellaneous materials that I use for more than one project. **Jewelry wire** is necessary for beading projects. Look for jewelry wire in the bead section of your local craft store, where you will find many styles and gauges of wire. Notice that the higher the gauge number, the thinner the wire. I've included the recommended gauge on the materials list for each project.

Fabric dye is a good material for softening colors and giving the projects a vintage look. My dye of choice is Rit Dye, available at craft stores and most supermarkets. I use tan most frequently, but there are many colors from which to choose. Many dye manufacturers even provide a mixing chart for creating custom colors.

Finally, some of the projects call for **wallpaper liner**. I use wallpaper liner as an economic alternative to store-bought interfacing. Available in hardware and home improvement stores, wallpaper liner comes on a large roll.

Acrylic spray finishes, jewelry wire, fabric dye and wallpaper liner are just some of the miscellaneous materials you will be using for the projects in this book.

Tools

Now that you have your materials, familiarize yourself with the tools you will need to complete the projects.

You will be using tools such as needle-nose pliers, a sewing machine and good scissors to craft stunning projects.

SEWING MACHINE

A sewing machine is required for only some of the projects. Fabrics of different weights require different needles, so make sure you have the correct needle for the fabric you are sewing. For example, in a few projects, you will be sewing more delicate fabrics, such as satin and silk; it is important to use the needle specified for that kind of fabric.

A seam allowance refers to the distance between the needle and the raw edge of the fabric. If you were making a quilt, your measurement would need to be exact, but for these projects, it is acceptable to approximate the distance. When the allowance is ¼" (6mm), I use the edge of the presser foot on my sewing machine as a guide. You can also follow the sewing machine guidemarks (if yours has them), or you can measure and place a piece of masking tape on the fabric to serve as a guide when feeding it through the machine.

When starting your seam, backstitch once or twice to anchor your thread. Repeat this when you have completed your seam. If you are new to machine stitching, refer to your sewing machine instruction book as a guide. I used 100% polyester thread for all the sewing machine projects and button thread for all the hand-stitching projects.

SCISSORS

Keep one pair of scissors for paper and another one for fabric. If you use the same pair on everything, they will get dull very quickly. Sharp scissors are a must, as they provide more accurate cuts and better results overall. Both paper and fabric scissors are available in decorative edges, such as pinking and scallop. Look for them in your local craft or fabric stores.

JEWELRY-MAKING TOOLS

Stock your crafting supply box with three pairs of pliers: needle-nose, flush cutter and wire crimper. You can use three-in-one pliers, which are available in the bead section of most craft stores. If you need a crash course in beading, I suggest picking up one of the many beading magazines available. Most provide "Beading 101" instructions and techniques that are thorough and helpful.

PART 1

Bridal Necklace

Bridal Tiara

Bridesmaid Bracelet

Flower Girl Headpiece

Flower Girl Pendant

Wedding Day Purse

For the Bride and Bridal Party

Nothing conveys classic romance better than a delicate vintage touch. In this section, you will find beautiful wearable projects for the bridal party—all with vintage charm. Some of the projects, like the Bridal Necklace and the Bridesmaid Bracelet, are simply constructed with crystals and beads. Others, like the Wedding Day Purse and the Flower Girl Headpiece, use softly dyed fabrics and flowers.

Mixing vintage style with glamour, these projects are a joy to make, give *and* wear. You can adorn yourself and your bridal party with these lovely accessories without having to learn complicated new techniques. With just a few basic beading and sewing skills, you will be able to create all the projects with ease.

Bridal Necklace

Something old, something new… To symbolize the bride's optimism and hope for the new life ahead of her, she is called by tradition to carry something new on her wedding day. Take charge of your own destiny and make the "something new" yourself. Create this beautiful necklace as a stunning accent to your wedding day attire. After the wedding is over, keep the necklace to remember the special day. Who knows—your handcrafted treasure may become a "something borrowed" for a close friend or "something old" for a bride of the next generation.

MATERIALS AND TOOLS

beads:

6mm crystal bicone beads

6mm pearl beads

5mm pearl beads

decorative silver-and-crystal slider beads (two kinds: rectangular and square)

round silver beads

decorative headpin

decorative silver jewelry finding

small jump ring

crimp tubes

10mm barrel clasps

26-gauge beading wire

wire crimpers

flush cutters

needle-nose pliers

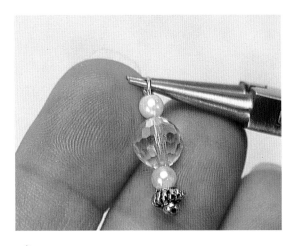

1 Make pendant

Thread a 6mm pearl bead, a crystal bead and another 6mm pearl bead onto a decorative headpin. Trim the headpin, leaving about ¼"–½" (6mm–13mm) of wire, then use pliers to curl the remaining wire into a small loop. Do not close the loop completely.

2 Add decorative jewelry finding

Add the decorative silver jewelry finding to the loop, then use the pliers to close the loop securely.

3 Add jump ring

Open a small jump ring and add it to the top loop of the jewelry finding.

4 Add wire and crystal to pendant

Cut two 36" (91cm) lengths of 26-gauge metal wire. Run the two pieces of wire together through the pendant jump ring, pulling them through until the lengths are even on either side. Gather the four ends of the wire together, then thread a crystal bead through the wire. Pull the bead down until it reaches the top of the pendant.

5 *Add beads and crystal slider*

Thread a 6mm pearl bead onto each pair of wires, pushing the pearls all the way down the wire to meet the crystal. Add a single rectangular silver-and-crystal slider bead, running each pair of wires through the corresponding set of holes on the slider.

6 *Continue beading*

Thread a 6mm pearl bead and a crystal bead onto each pair of wires. Proceed with the right side of the necklace first, adding a single rectangular silver-and-crystal slider bead, running the individual wires through the corresponding set of holes on the slider.

7 *Add more beads*

Thread two 5mm pearl beads and one 6mm pearl bead onto each individual wire, then add a square silver-and-crystal slider bead, running the wires through the corresponding set of holes on the slider.

8 *Add pearls and slider bead*

Add one 6mm pearl bead to each individual wire, followed by two 5mm pearl beads, one crystal bead, two more 5mm pearl beads and one more crystal bead. Add another rectangular silver-and-crystal slider bead.

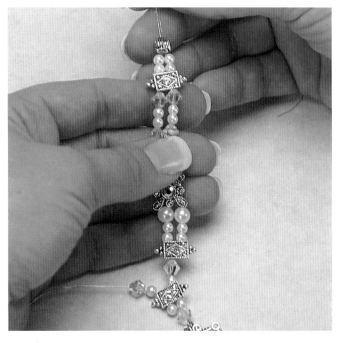

9 Finish beading progression

Add two 6mm pearl beads to each individual wire, then thread a single round silver bead over both wires.

10 Add pearl beads

Begin threading pearl beads over the two wires, alternating one 5mm pearl between every two 6mm pearls. Follow this pattern four times.

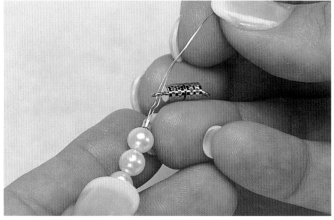

12 Add clasp

Slide a crimp tube and barrel clasp onto the end of the wire. Trim the remaining wire, leaving about ¾" (2cm).

11 Finish adding pearls

Add eighteen more 6mm pearl beads to the two wires, finishing up the right side of the necklace.

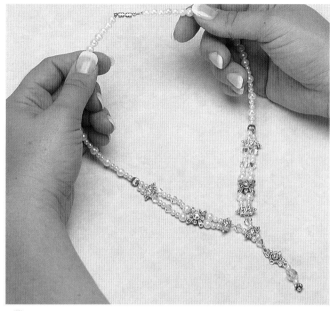

13 Crimp bead

Using needle-nose pliers, loop the wire back through the crimp tube and into the first pearl bead, eliminating any slack in the wire. When the wire end has gone far enough, secure it by crimping the tube with the wire crimpers.

14 Finish left side of necklace

Bead the left side of the necklace, following the same beading progression so it mirrors the right side. Add a crimping tube and barrel clasp to the end of the wire. Secure the wire by crimping the tube, as you did in step 13.

{ ANOTHER ROMANTIC IDEA }

After you have made the bridal necklace, this bracelet will be a snap to assemble. Follow the same general assembly pattern as the necklace, adding pearl, crystal and slider beads as you desire.

Bridal Tiara

With crystals interspersed among its elegant double strands of pearls, this bridal tiara looks so beautiful that nobody will believe you made it yourself. And you won't believe how simple it is to create—that can be your little secret! All you need for this project is a comb-in headband, some wire and a supply of beads and crystals. By simply stringing beads and wrapping the wire around the bridal frame, you will create a graceful look fit for the most sophisticated of brides.

MATERIALS AND TOOLS

plain wire comb-in headband

beads:

round silver beads

5mm pearl beads

8mm pearl beads

6mm bicone crystal beads

decorative silver-and-crystal slider beads (rectangular)

crimp bead or tube

beading wire,
24-gauge and 32-gauge

wire crimpers

flush cutters

needle-nose pliers

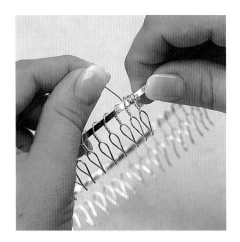

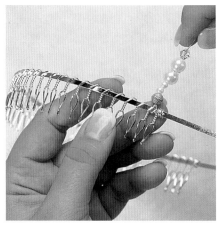

1 Anchor wire to head band

Cut a 36" (91cm) length of 24-gauge wire. Anchor one end of the wire to the headband by wrapping it three times around the end tooth of the comb.

2 Add beads

Add the first series of beads onto the wire, following this progression: one silver bead, two 5mm pearl beads, two 8mm pearl beads, one crystal bead, two 8mm pearl beads, two 5mm pearl beads, one silver bead.

3 Finish first upper scallop

Form the beaded wire into an arch. Bring it down to meet the 7th or 8th tooth of the comb, then wrap it around the tooth a few times. Once the first scallop is secure, you can adjust the shape of the arch.

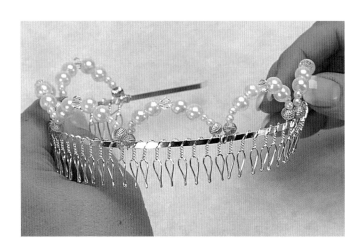

4 Finish upper scallops

Continue beading the wire, following the same progression of beads and securing each scallop to the headband as described in steps 2–3. Wrap the remaining wire around the frame to secure it, then trim the leftover wire. When complete, you should have six beaded scallops, as shown.

5 Anchor second length of wire

Cut a 30" (76cm) length of 32-gauge wire. Wrap the wire around the headband, directly below the first bead of the first scallop, then anchor the 32-gauge wire by looping it around the 24-gauge wire. Pull the 32-gauge wire through until its two tails are equal in length.

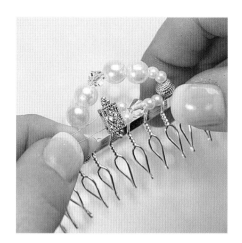  

6 Add beads to wire

Hold the two tails of wire together, then slide on two 5mm pearl beads and one crystal bead. Separate the two tails, then add a 5mm pearl bead onto each tail. Add a rectangular silver-and-crystal slider bead, running each tail through the corresponding set of holes on the slider.

7 Finish beading lower scallop

Finish beading the first lower scallop, adding one 5mm pearl bead onto each tail followed by one crystal bead and three 5mm pearl beads onto both tails together. Shape the beaded wire into an arch directly underneath the first scallop.

8 Secure first lower scallop

Wrap the wire once around the headband between the two silver end beads of the upper layer of beaded scallops.

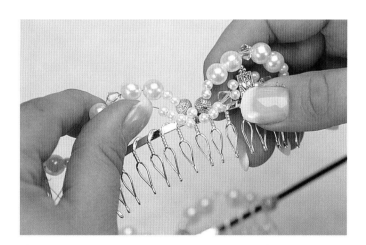 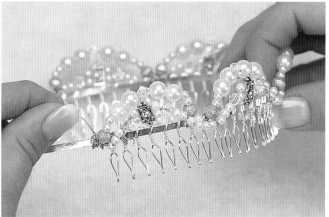

9 Add more pearl beads

After you've wrapped the wire around the headband, add one more 5mm pearl bead. Wrap the wire around the headband again, then add two more 5mm pearl beads. Add another series of beads, following the progression described in steps 6–7. Form the beaded wire into another scallop, secure the wire, and continue with another scallop.

10 Finish tiara

Finish the tiara by repeating the same pattern until you have completed a lower row of six scallops. When finished, secure the remaining wire by wrapping it around the headband several times. Loop it and tie it in a knot, then trim the excess wire. For extra security, use crimpers to finish the wire with a crimping bead or tube before trimming the wire.

Bridesmaid Bracelet

Surprise your bridesmaids with this beautiful handcrafted bracelet. With its delicate design, this bracelet will look lovely gracing the wrists of your dearest friends. You can change the color of the crystals to match the bridesmaids' gowns, or you can personalize them by making each one slightly different. While bridesmaids' gowns might hang in the closet long after the wedding day, these bracelets can be worn over and over again!

MATERIALS AND TOOLS

beads:

4mm bicone crystal beads

4mm bicone light sapphire beads

6mm bicone crystal beads

mix of decorative silver-and-crystal slider beads (round and/or square)

crimp tubes (or crimp beads)

barrel clasp

26-gauge beading wire

wire crimpers

flush cutters

needle-nose pliers

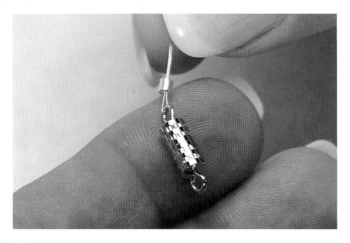

1 Cut wire and add barrel clasp

Cut a 30" (76cm) length of 26-gauge wire. Run the wire through one end loop of a barrel clasp, then bend the wire in half. Holding the two ends of the wire together, slide a crimp tube (or crimp bead) down to the loop, then crimp the tube with wire crimpers.

2 Add crystals

Holding the two ends of the wire together, slide on three crystal beads, beginning with a 4mm crystal, followed by a 4mm light sapphire crystal, then a 6mm crystal.

3 Add beads to each wire

Separate the two ends of the wire. Add two 4mm light sapphire crystal beads and one 6mm crystal bead to each individual wire. Add a decorative silver-and-crystal slider bead, running each wire through the corresponding set of holes on the slider.

4 Continue beading

Add one 6mm crystal bead, three 4mm sapphire crystal beads and one more 6mm crystal bead to each individual wire. Add another silver-and-crystal slider bead, running each wire through the corresponding set of holes on the slider.

5 Add center accent beads

Add one 6mm crystal bead and one 4mm light sapphire crystal bead to each individual wire. Add a different silver-and-crystal slider bead as the center accent piece, running each wire through the corresponding set of holes on the slider.

6 Complete beading

Finish beading the bracelet, mirroring the progression of beads on the other side of the center crystal slider.

7 Cut wire and add crimping bead

Cut the remaining wire, leaving approximately ½" (13mm) on each end. Slide a crimp tube (or crimp bead) over the wire.

8 Finish with barrel clasp

Run the wire ends through the other end loop of the barrel clasp. Pull the wire through the loop, then insert the wire ends into the crimp tube (or crimp bead). Feed the remainder of the wire through the crimp tube to eliminate slack, then crimp the tube with wire crimpers to secure.

Flower Girl Headpiece

Wearing this sweet crown of blossoms, your flower girl will feel like a little princess on your wedding day. You can use fabric dye to give the headpiece a very light hue for a soft, Victorian look, or you can choose to keep it white or ivory. If you want to create an entirely different look, dye the flowers to coordinate with the bridal bouquet. Whatever style you choose, the headpiece is bound to make your flower girl look especially charming.

MATERIALS AND TOOLS

round headpiece form,
to fit flower girl's head

hem tape *(Oyster 028)*

small silk flowers, with stems:

> *white*

> *ivory*

> *light pink*

> *dark pink*

scissors

hot glue gun and glue sticks

fabric dye *(tan or ecru)*

plastic tub, for mixing dye

towel

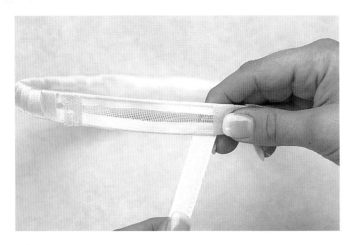

1 Wrap headpiece form with hem tape

Use hot glue to adhere one end of the hem tape to the headpiece form. Wrap the tape around the form until it is entirely
covered. When finished, cut the hem tape and hot glue the end
to the form.

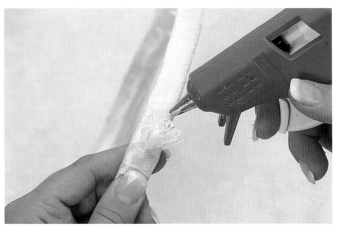

2 Attach silk flowers

Trim the stems of the white and ivory silk flowers to about 1½"
(4cm). Insert a flower into the headpiece form, slipping the stems
between the edges of the wrapped hem tape. Secure the flower in
place with hot glue.

3 Cover headpiece with flowers

Continue adding ivory and white silk flowers to the headpiece
form, securing each with hot glue. Place the flowers close together
to cover the entire ring.

4 Dye headpiece

Prepare a batch of tan or ecru fabric dye according to the package
instructions. Dip the entire headpiece into the dye, submerging
for only two or three seconds (see *Tip*, page 31). When you
remove the headpiece, it should be a very light tan.

5 Dry headpiece

Place the headpiece on a towel, then gently pat it dry. Allow the headpiece to air dry completely.

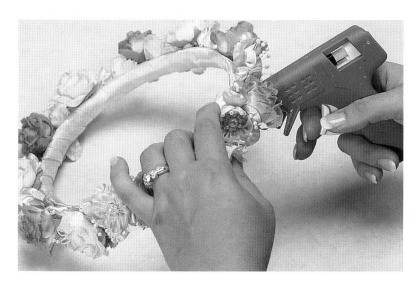

6 Add pink flowers

Add light and dark pink silk flowers to the headpiece, spacing them evenly around the ring and securing them in place with hot glue.

TIP   FABRIC DYE SUCH AS RIT can be used to dye several kinds of embellishments. Silk flowers, ribbon, beads and many kinds of fabric can be dyed. Simply prepare the dye formula according to the package instructions, then submerge the object in the dye for a very short period of time, usually only a couple of seconds. Be conservative when you are dying an object. Remember—you can always make the object darker by dipping it again, but you can't make it lighter!

Flower Girl Pendant

Made with just a few simple materials—a length of organza ribbon, a handful of pearls and a single letter sticker—this personalized pendant makes the perfect accessory for young flower girls. Even your tiniest attendant will enjoy wearing this charming necklace, and she'll love having it for future "dress-up" occasions!

MATERIALS AND TOOLS

1 yard (91 cm) pink sheer organza ribbon, 1" (3cm) wide

8mm pearl beads

metal pendant frame

oval dimensional resin alphabet sticker, with initial of flower girl's name *(to fit inside pendant frame)*

32-gauge beading wire

scissors

permanent adhesive glue

flush cutters

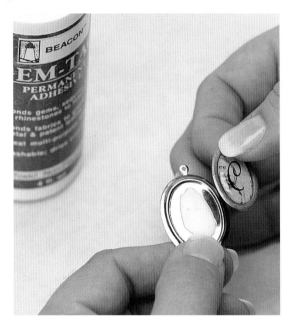

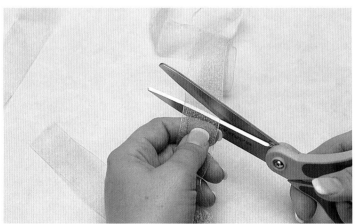

2 Cut ribbon

Cut approximately 24" (61cm) of pink organza ribbon.

1 Make pendant

Use permanent adhesive glue to attach the oval monogram sticker to the pendant frame.

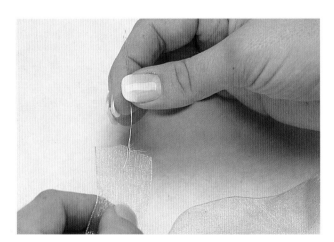

3 Thread ribbon onto wire needle

Cut a 6" (15cm) length of 32-gauge wire and run it through one end of the organza ribbon. This will function as a needle for threading objects onto the ribbon.

4 Add pendant

Slip the pendant over the wire needle and onto the ribbon. Position the pendant at the center of the ribbon.

5 Tie knot

Secure the pendant in place by tying the ribbon in a knot.

6 Add pearl bead

Thread the first pearl bead onto one end of the ribbon, placing it 1½" (4cm) from the pendant.

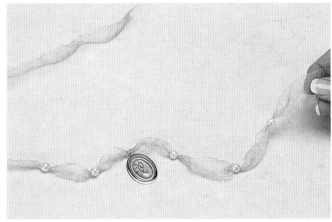

7 Add two more pearl beads

Thread two more pearl beads onto the same side of the ribbon, placing them 1½" (4cm) apart from each other.

8 Complete other side

Thread three pearl beads onto the other end of the ribbon, sliding them into position to mirror the beads on the opposite side. Once on the ribbon, the beads should stay in place without having to be adhered with glue.

Wedding Day Purse

Every bride needs a purse to carry her "emergency supplies"—some bobby pins, a bit of makeup and, of course, a handkerchief. Consider making one purse for yourself and one purse as a gift for each of your bridesmaids. With its soft beiges and creams, this purse will be a gorgeous complement to any bride's or bridesmaid's gown.

MATERIALS AND TOOLS

pencil and heavy paper,
for pattern

fabric:

½ yard (46cm) taupe bridal satin

*½ yard (46cm) ivory bridal satin,
plus 4" (10 cm) more for strip*

1 yard (91cm) scallop ivory lace,
¾" (2cm) wide

½ yard (46cm) ivory ribbon,
1" (3cm) wide

1 yard (91cm) ivory cord

½ yard (46cm) crystal-beaded fringe

beads:

8mm pearl beads

6mm pearl beads

pink ribbon roses

white silk leaves

scissors

fabric glue

hot glue gun and glue sticks

needle and taupe or ivory
button thread

disappearing ink marker

pins

chopstick or other pointed object

iron

photocopier

sewing machine

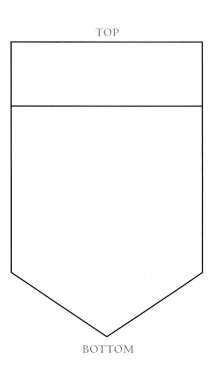

TOP

BOTTOM

PURSE PATTERN

Use a photocopier to enlarge this pattern 200%. Enlarge the pattern again at 150% to bring to full size. Cut out the pattern, then trace it onto a sheet of heavy paper. Cut the pattern out of the heavy paper and use it for steps 1 and 4.

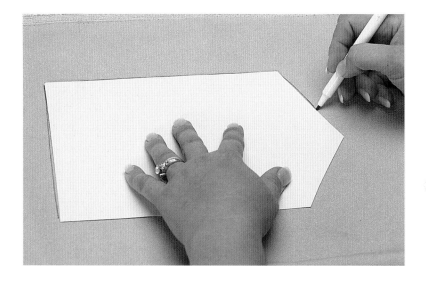

1 Trace pattern onto taupe satin

Fold the taupe satin in half so the right sides of the fabric are on the inside and the wrong sides face out. With a disappearing ink marker, trace the pattern onto one side of the fabric facing out.

2 Stitch satin

Machine stitch along the lines of the pattern, stitching the two sides of the satin together. Stitch along all the pattern lines except the top, which should be left open.

Note: Make sure you have the appropriate needle on your sewing machine for satin (typically a 9 or 11, or universal).

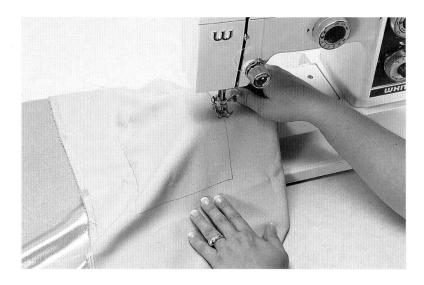

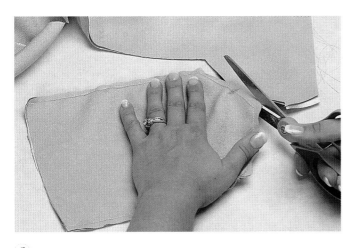

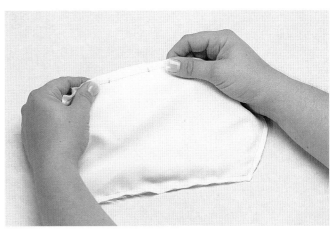

3 Cut out purse

Trim outside the seam, allowing ⅛"–¼" (3mm–6mm) around the stitched edges. Cut right along the unstitched top edge.

Note: Satin will naturally fray when it is cut.

4 Cut and stitch ivory satin

Repeat steps 1–3 for the ivory satin. When tracing the pattern onto the fabric, mark off a 2" (5cm) length along one of the long sides, as shown. Leave these 2" (5cm) unstitched so you can turn the fabric in step 7.

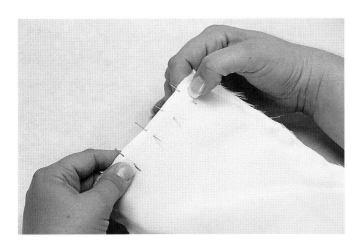

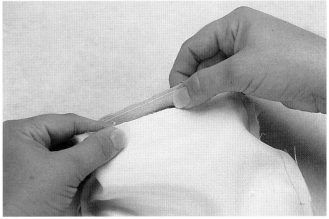

5 Fit bags together

Turn the taupe satin bag right side out, then fit the taupe bag inside the ivory bag. The right sides of the satin bags should now be facing each other. Slip your hand into the opening of the taupe bag, separating the two sides of the purse along the top edges. Pin the taupe satin to the ivory satin along the top edge on one side of the purse, and the taupe satin to the ivory satin on the other side, as shown.

6 Stitch bags together

Leaving a ¼" (6mm) seam allowance, stitch the top edge of the taupe and ivory bags on one pinned side, removing the pins as you sew. Stitch the top edges of the bags together on the other pinned side in the same fashion. Trim the fabric just outside the seam, allowing ⅛" (3mm) along the stitched edges and cutting off any frayed ends. The bags should now be connected along the two edges of the top opening.

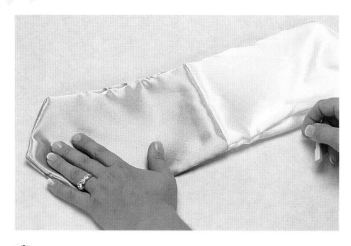

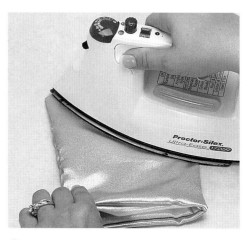

7 Turn fabric right side out

Pull the material right side out through the 2" (5cm) opening. The two bags should now be connected as one, as shown. Insert a chopstick or other pointed object into the opening and push the tip into each corner, forcing out the material to form pointed corners. Hand stitch the 2" (5cm) opening closed with thread.

8 Insert ivory bag

Insert the ivory bag inside the taupe bag. Iron the taupe satin carefully.

9 Cut ivory satin strip

Cut a 2" × 12½" (5cm x 32cm) strip of ivory satin.

10 Attach ivory strip

Pin the ivory satin strip along the top of the purse, about ¾" (19mm) from the top edge. Machine stitch the ivory satin to the purse, stitching about ⅛" (3mm) in from the top and bottom of the strip.

11 Attach lace

Using fabric glue, attach a 1"-wide (3cm) ivory ribbon along the center of the ivory satin strip. Then, glue lengths of ivory scallop lace along the top and bottom of the strip, covering the raw edges of the fabric. Bring the ribbon and the lace around the bag, trimming any overlapping ends to meet.

12 Add decorative ribbon to bottom

Use fabric glue to adhere beaded fringe along the bottom edges of the purse. Run the fringe along the front and back edges, then trim it where the two ends meet in front.

13 Attach purse strap

Use hot glue to attach the ends of the ivory cord to the inside of each corner, creating a shoulder strap.

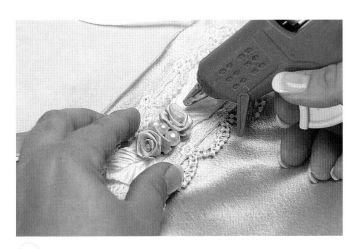

14 Add decorative treatment to top

With a hot glue gun, add a cluster of ribbon roses, silk leaves and pearl beads at the center of the ribbon along the top of the purse. *Note: If you have white ribbon roses, you can dye them pink or another soft color with fabric dye, such as Rit. See Tip, page 31, for more instruction.*

15 Add decorative treatment to bottom

Use hot glue to add a small cluster of ribbon roses and pearl beads to the bottom center point, covering the ends of the beaded-fringe ribbon.

PART 2

Wedding Invitations
Church Door Ornament
Bouquet Cuff
Unity Candle Set
Ceremony Program
Flower Girl Basket
Ring Bearer Pillow

For the Ceremony

After weeks, months and maybe even years of preparation, you're ready for the big moment when you say, "I do." The ceremony, especially the exchange of vows, is the most important and most meaningful part of your wedding day. Are you looking for ways to make your ceremony truly unforgettable? If so, consider the elegant projects in this section.

These projects make charming accent pieces for any wedding ceremony. They all complement one another, which means everything—from the romantic Church Door Ornament to the elegant Ceremony Program— will have a tailored look that is uniquely your own. To inject your own style into the projects, use papers, ribbons and embellishments of your choosing.

Wedding Invitations

Featuring the colors, words and design of your choice, invitations set the tone for your wedding and let your guests know what to expect. After receiving this handcrafted invitation, they will anticipate an affair nothing less than exquisite. Select coordinating papers that represent your individual style. You may opt to incorporate your wedding colors or perhaps an image or motif that your friends and family associate with you and your husband-to-be. Check with the post office before sending out these invitations, as the unusual dimensions may affect the cost of postage.

MATERIALS AND TOOLS

pencil and heavy paper,
for pattern

colored cardstock:
  robin's egg blue

  ivory

  pink

blue floral decorative paper
(*Anna Griffin AG 147*)

pink vellum paper

½ yard (46 cm) pink ribbon,
¼" (6mm) wide

small pink ribbon bow

scissors

decorative-edged scissors

metal ruler

paper glue

bone folder

computer and printer

photocopier

OPTIONAL:
  ribbon punch

INVITATION PATTERN

Use a photocopier to enlarge this pattern 200%. Enlarge the pattern again at 106% to bring to full size. Cut out the pattern, then trace it onto a sheet of heavy paper. Cut the pattern out of the heavy paper and use it for steps 1–2.

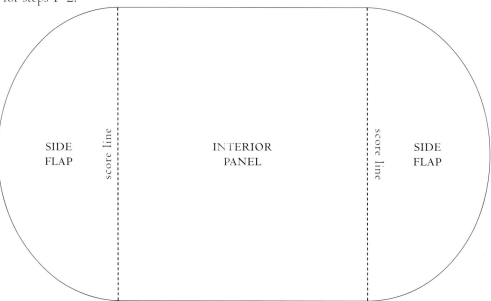

SIDE FLAP   score line   INTERIOR PANEL   score line   SIDE FLAP

1 Cut out cardstock

Trace the pattern onto robin's egg blue cardstock and cut it out.

2 Cut out decorative paper

Trace the pattern onto decorative paper and cut it out with straight scissors. Line up the edge of a metal ruler with one of the score lines, then run a bone folder along the edge to score the paper from top to bottom. Repeat with the other score line, then fold both side flaps in. Use decorative-edged scissors to cut the rounded ends of the flaps, trimming about ¼" (6mm) off the edges.

3 Glue decorative paper to cardstock

Use a metal ruler and bone folder to score the lines on the blue cardstock, as described in the previous step. Fold the side flaps in. Glue the decorative paper to the exterior of the cardstock, as shown.

4 Add decorative interior panel

Cut a 5½" x 6¼" (14cm x 16cm) sheet of decorative paper to fit the interior panel of the card. Glue the paper to the panel.

5 Create invitation panel

Use a computer to design and print your invitation text on ivory cardstock, containing the text within a 3" x 3½" (8cm x 9cm) area. Cut the cardstock around the text, trimming to a 3½" x 4" (9cm x 10cm) panel. Cut two robin's egg blue cardstock borders, each measuring 3½" x 1½" (9cm x 4cm), then trim one long end of each border piece with decorative-edged scissors. Glue the borders to the back of the ivory cardstock, allowing a ½" (13mm) decorative edge to show along the top and bottom.

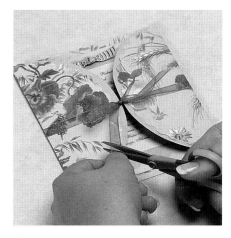

6 Glue invitation panel to interior

Glue the invitation text, border included, to a sheet of pink cardstock measuring 4" x 5½" (10cm x 14cm). Center the invitation panel on the decorative interior panel and glue in place.

7 Add vellum and bow

Add a dab of glue at the upper center of the invitation panel, then adhere a 4" x 5½" (10cm x 14cm) sheet of pink vellum paper over the invitation, lining up the edges. Adhere a small pink bow over the glue spot.

Note: Another option is to make two holes with a ribbon punch, then secure the vellum to the panel by running a piece of ribbon through the holes and tying it in a small bow.

8 Close flaps with ribbon

Close the front flaps of the invitation, then tie a ribbon around it to keep the flaps closed. Tie a bow in front and trim the ends of the ribbon as necessary.

Church Door Ornament

Hearts have always been used to symbolize romance and love. To announce the celebration of your love, hang a monogrammed heart on the door of the church. If you like, you can make two hearts, one bearing the monogram of the groom and the other the monogram of the bride. Pretty corsage pins serve as great anchors to hold the fabric to the foam heart base—no sewing required! Complete the look with matching pew ornaments, giving smaller foam hearts the same decorative treatment.

MATERIALS AND TOOLS

10" (25cm) foam heart

pencil and heavy paper,
for pattern

fabric:
   ¾ yard (69cm) taupe bridal satin

   ½ yard (46cm) oatmeal wool felt

quilt batting

2½ yards (2.3m) cream ribbon,
1" (3cm) wide

pearl beads, any size

pink clay flowers with pips

ivory silk flowers

corsage pins

scissors

hot glue gun and glue sticks

disappearing ink marker

computer with fancy font, such as
Edwardian, and printer

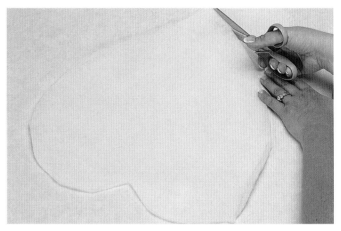

1 *Trace and cut out satin heart*

Trace around the foam heart on a sheet of heavy paper. Cut the paper heart out and use it as a pattern. Lay the taupe bridal satin on your work surface with the wrong side facing up. Place the paper pattern on the satin, then use a disappearing ink marker to trace 2" (5cm) beyond the perimeter of the pattern, as shown. Cut the satin, following along the marker lines.

2 *Cut quilt batting*

Place the paper pattern on the quilt batting, then use a disappearing ink marker to trace 2" (5cm) beyond the perimeter of the pattern, as in step 1. Cut the batting, following along the lines.

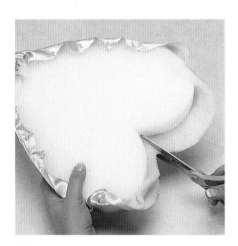

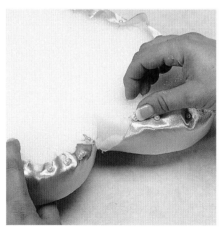

3 *Pin satin and batting to foam*

Center the quilt batting and satin on the foam heart, with the right side of the satin facing out. Pull the batting and the satin around the edges of the heart and temporarily secure the fabric in place with corsage pins, keeping it taut. Before pinning the upper section of the heart, cut the satin and batting to meet the upper center point of the heart, as shown.

4 *Finish pinning*

Finish pinning the batting and the satin to the heart. When you come to the center point, do not worry about the exposed foam; this will be covered in steps 6–7. After the pinning is complete, tack the pinned satin to the back of the foam heart with hot glue.

5 *Cover back of foam*

Using the paper pattern from step 1, trace the heart shape onto a piece of oatmeal wool felt. Cut out the felt heart, then place it over the back of the foam heart. Secure the felt in place with corsage pins, inserting each pin at an angle through the felt, satin and batting as you remove the existing pin. Continue pinning until all the raw edges are covered and the satin is taut.

6 Attach ribbon

Attach the cream ribbon around the edge of the foam heart by inserting corsage pins directly through the center of the ribbon and into the foam. Start the ribbon at the top center point of the heart, bringing the ribbon all the way around the perimeter, then trim the ribbon where the two ends meet. At this same point, create a simple bow by making a loop with the ribbon and pinning the center with a corsage pin, as shown.

7 Add bow and handle

Cut a 36" (91 cm) length of the same cream ribbon used in step 6. Fashion a looped handle, then pin it securely in place at the top center point of the heart. Arrange silk flowers, clay flowers and pearl beads in a decorative cluster at the top of the heart. Hot glue the embellishments in place.

8 Design and attach monogram

With a computer and printer, design, enlarge and print the letter of your choice, using the desired font. Cut out the printed letter, then use a disappearing ink marker to trace around it onto the oatmeal wool felt. Cut out the felt letter, then center it on the front of the heart. Secure the letter in place with evenly spaced corsage pins.

9 Glue flowers and beads to bottom point

Arrange silk flowers, clay flowers and pearl beads in a decorative cluster at the bottom of the heart. Hot glue the embellishments in place.

{ANOTHER ROMANTIC IDEA}

If you like the look of the Church Door Ornament, why not carry the theme a step further? Make smaller hearts in the style of the door ornament, then hang them on the ends of the pews or rows of seats. Your aisle will be lined with lovely matching hearts!

Bouquet Cuff

Sometimes little details, like intricate beadwork on a dress or soft candles lighting the room, make all the difference. Add an elegant, finishing detail to the wedding bouquets by wrapping the stems in complementary bouquet cuffs. Choose fabrics that coordinate with the colors and styles of the arrangements that the bride and bridesmaids will be carrying. A bouquet cuff can be as fancy or as understated as you like. And not only does it look pretty, it makes the bouquets easier to carry!

MATERIALS AND TOOLS

pencil and heavy paper, for pattern

floral bouquet

¼ yard (23cm) fabric *(color and pattern to complement bouquet)*

wallpaper liner or stiff interfacing

1 yard (91cm) cream ribbon, 1" (3cm) wide

6mm pearl beads

corsage pins

scissors

hot glue gun and glue sticks

chopstick or other pointed object

disappearing ink marker

iron

sewing machine

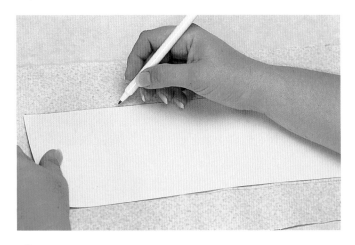

1 Trace pattern onto fabric

Cut an 11½" x 4" (29cm x 10cm) rectangular pattern from heavy paper. Fold the fabric in half so the right sides of the fabric are on the inside and the wrong sides face out. With a disappearing ink marker, trace the pattern onto one side of the fabric facing out.

2 Stitch fabric

Machine stitch the folded fabric along the traced lines, leaving one short end unstitched; this opening will allow you to turn the fabric in the next step. Trim outside the seam, allowing ⅛" (3mm) around the stitched edges. Cut right along the unstitched edge.

3 Turn fabric

Stick your hand through the opening and grab the end of the fabric pocket, turning it inside out.

4 Point corners

Insert a chopstick or other pointed object into the opening and push the tip into the bottom corners of the pocket, forcing out the material to form pointed corners.

5 Insert liner into pocket

Press the fabric well with a warm iron. Trace the rectangular pattern from step 1 onto a piece of wallpaper liner or stiff interfacing, then cut it out. Slip the liner inside the opening and insert it into the stitched pocket. (You might need to bend the liner to make it fit.) Trim the end of the liner if necessary.

6 Fold in edges

Use an iron to press the fabric pocket with the wallpaper liner inside. Fold the top raw edges in about ½" (13mm), then press the fabric one more time.

7 Stitch cuff

Machine stitch the opening closed, then continue around the entire cuff, stitching ⅛" (3mm) in from each edge.

8 Wrap and secure cuff

Wrap the cuff around the floral bouquet. Adjust the cuff so that the ends are placed at the back of the bouquet. When the cuff is in place, secure it with a corsage pin. You can add hot glue for extra security.

9 Tie bow around cuff and add embellishments

Tie the cream ribbon around the center of the cuff with a bow in the front. Trim the ends of the ribbon into "V" shapes. Determine the placement of six pearl beads on the cuff, three above the bow and three below. Mark the placement with a disappearing ink marker, then hot glue the pearls in place.

{ANOTHER ROMANTIC IDEA}

You can make a bouquet cuff for all your bridesmaids. For a little variety, slightly alter the design and/or fabric of each cuff, like the ones pictured here.

Unity Candle Set

Many wedding ceremonies include the tradition of lighting a unity candle to symbolize the union of two lives. Two lit taper candles represent the separate lives of the bride and groom, and an unlit pillar candle in the center represents their lives together. During the ceremony, the bride and groom use the taper candles to light the pillar candle, an outward sign of their inward commitment. Make the intimate display of this tradition even more meaningful by making your own simply and romantically decorated unity candle and candleholders.

MATERIALS AND TOOLS

FOR THE CANDLE:

white or ivory candle,
9" (23cm) high

white or ivory Venetian lace collar

white or ivory scalloped lace trim

Swarovski crystal accents

decorative medallion
(scrapbook embellishment by Hirschberg Schutz & Co. Inc.)

corsage pins

scissors

permanent adhesive glue

needle-nose pliers

FOR THE CANDLEHOLDERS:

two crystal candleholders,
with wide, round bases

decorative ribbon

8mm pearl beads

small pink silk ribbon roses

scissors

flush cutters

hot glue gun and glue sticks,
or glass glue

Ceremony Candle

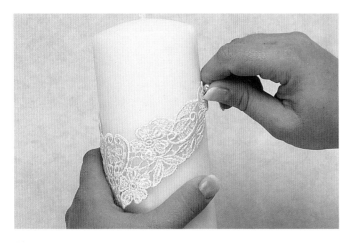

1 Attach lace collar to candle

Position the lace collar on the candle, placing the ends about 2¼" (6cm) from the top. Secure the collar to the candle with corsage pins, inserting the pins all the way into the candle until just the pearl ends are visible. To push the pins into the candle, you may need to use needle-nose pliers.

2 Add lace trim along top

Place a length of scalloped lace trim along the top of the candle, positioning it about ¼" (6mm) from the edge. Secure the lace in place with corsage pins.

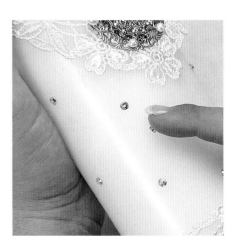

3 Add lace trim along bottom

Place a length of scalloped lace trim along the bottom of the candle, positioning it about ¼" (6mm) from the edge. Secure the lace in place with corsage pins.

4 Add embellishment

Place the decorative medallion in the center of the lace collar, allowing the lace to frame its edges. Secure the medallion to the candle with six corsage pins.

5 Add crystals

Glue crystal accents to the candle with permanent adhesive glue, spacing them evenly from top to bottom.

Candleholder

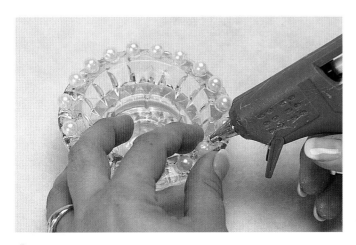

1 Add pearl beads to rim

Hot glue 8mm pearl beads along the top rim of the candleholder, spacing them evenly.

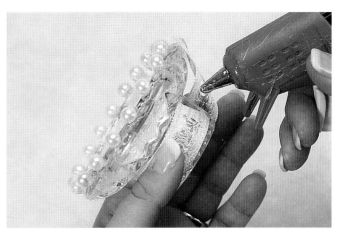

2 Wrap base with ribbon

Wrap a decorative ribbon around the base of the candleholder, trimming where the two ends meet. Secure the ribbon to the base with hot glue or glass glue.

TIP ADD OLD-FASHIONED CHARM by using pieces of vintage jewelry as embellishments for the candles.

3 Trim flower stems

Use flush cutters to trim the wire stems of several small silk ribbon roses, leaving about ¼" (6mm) of wire.

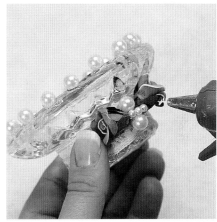

4 Add embellishments

Hot glue the silk ribbon roses and a few pearl beads in a cluster at the base of the candleholder, covering the area where the ribbon ends meet.

Ceremony Program

The wedding program welcomes your guests to the ceremony and also captures the spirit of the celebration. The graceful style of this program conveys bridal elegance. On the inside, there is a pocket to hold a thoughtful favor for your guests. Why not surprise them with a lace handkerchief, a vellum envelope filled with rose petals, or a packet of birdseed to shower upon the newlyweds?

MATERIALS AND TOOLS

yellow/blue floral decorative paper *(Anna Griffin AG 069)*

cardstock:
  light blue

  white or ivory

¾ yard (69cm) light blue decorative ribbon, ¼" (6mm) wide

white or ivory button, ½" (13mm) diameter

scissors

decorative-edged scissors

metal ruler

paper glue

hot glue gun and glue sticks

bone folder

silver eyelets

hammer, eyelet punch and eyelet setter

computer and printer

OPTIONAL (for pocket favor):

  vellum envelope

  lace handkerchief

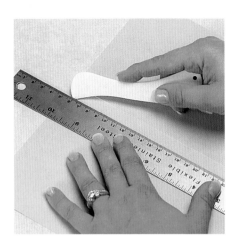

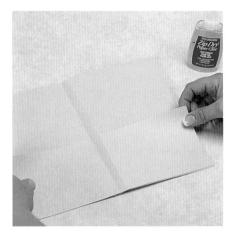

1 Measure and score cardstock

Place an 8½" x 11" (22cm x 28cm) sheet of light blue cardstock horizontally on your work surface. Measure in 5¼" (13cm) from the right side, then use a bone folder to score a vertical line from top to bottom. Repeat on the left side, measuring in 5¼" (13cm) and scoring a vertical line.

2 Cut and glue decorative paper

Cut a sheet of decorative paper to 8½" x 11" (22cm x 28cm). Glue the paper onto the front of the light blue cardstock. Rescore the paper to reinforce the score lines made in step 1.

3 Create inside pocket

Cut a 4" x 11" (10cm x 28cm) strip of the same light blue cardstock used in step 1. Open up the card and position the strip along the bottom, lining up the edges. Adhere the strip to create a pocket, applying glue just around the side and bottom edges.

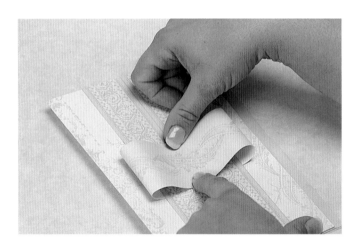

4 Begin paper bow on cover

Cut a 2" x 6½" (5cm x 17cm) strip of the same decorative paper used in step 2. Bring the ends of the paper strip together to form a loop, then position it, centered, on the front cover of the program. Once you have determined the placement, add a dab of glue on the front side of one end of the strip and adhere it to the front cover. Loop the strip over, add another dab of glue on the front side of the other end, and adhere. Add glue beneath the center of the loop and press the paper down to adhere it.

5 Finish bow and add paper embellishment

Cut a 2" x 3¾" (5cm x 10cm) strip of the same decorative paper. Bring the ends of the strip together, then glue in place to form a small loop. Glue this loop onto the center of the loop already adhered to the program cover. This should create the look of a paper bow. Next, use decorative-edged scissors to cut a 2¼" x 3¾" (6cm x 10cm) oval out of white or ivory cardstock. Fold the oval in half lengthwise, then place it over the top edge of the front cover. Glue the oval in place.

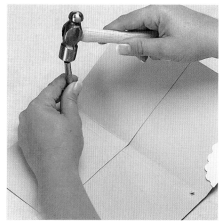

6 Create eyelets

Use an eyelet punch and hammer to make two eyelet holes along the spine of the cover, placing one about ½" (13mm) from the top and the other about ½" (13mm) from the bottom.

7 Set eyelets

Use an eyelet setter to set eyelets in the holes on the spine.

8 Insert program

Design and print your wedding ceremony program text on white or ivory cardstock. Fold the program in half, then punch two holes along the fold to correspond with the eyelets on the cover. Line up the holes, then run a decorative ribbon through them, so both ends of the ribbon are on the inside of the program. Tie the ribbon in a bow to secure the interior program to the cover.

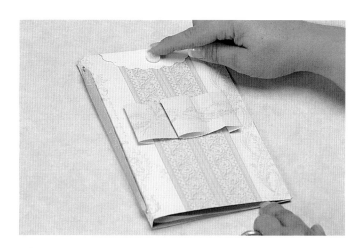

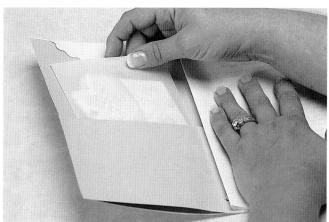

9 Add button embellishment

Hot glue a white or ivory button to the front of the program cover, centering it on the half-oval at the top.

10 Insert favor into program pocket

Insert a ceremony favor into the interior pocket of the program. Here, I've created a simple favor by tucking a lace handkerchief into a vellum envelope.

Flower Girl Basket

Nothing is quite so captivating as a beautiful flower girl throwing petals as she walks down the aisle. Send her on her way in style by crafting this pretty pink flower girl basket. To make the basket, you might use old heirloom lace from your family, or purchase elegant lace from your local fabric and craft stores. Carrying such a lovely accessory, your little attendant will feel like the star of the show—so don't be surprised if she steals a scene or two!

MATERIALS AND TOOLS

metal bucket (with handle),
4" (10cm) high and
4½" (11cm) wide

fabric:
   ½ yard (46cm) white or ivory
   bridal satin

   ¼ yard (23cm) oatmeal wool felt

   ½ yard (46cm) pink tulle

½ yard (46cm) delicate lace
or vintage hand-crocheted lace,
4" (10cm) wide

½ yard (46cm) lace trim,
½" (13mm) wide

1 yard (91cm) decorative ribbon,
½" (13mm) wide

8mm ivory or pink pearl beads

light and dark pink silk roses

18" (46cm) length of
18-gauge floral stem wire

scissors

hot glue gun and glue sticks

flush cutters

needle-nose pliers

flowers or flower petals,
to fill the basket

1 Cover bucket with satin

Remove the handle from the metal bucket. Hot glue white or ivory bridal satin along the top edge of the bucket, placing the fabric flush with the edge. Bring the satin all the way around the bucket to cover the entire surface. Fold under any remaining satin, then hot glue it to the surface to make a seam, as shown.

2 Glue satin to bottom

Tuck the excess satin on the bottom under the bucket, pulling taut. Secure the satin with hot glue.

3 Cover bottom with felt

Cut a circular piece of oatmeal wool felt slightly smaller than the bottom surface of the bucket. Hot glue the felt onto the bucket bottom to hide the raw edges of the cut satin.

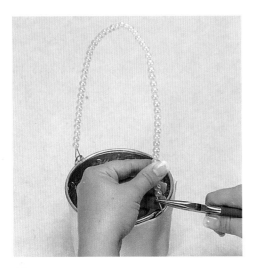

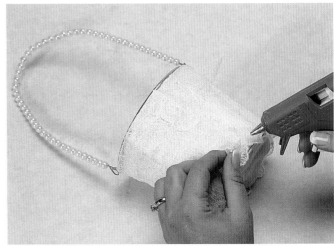

4 Add handle

With the needle-nose pliers, grip the 18-gauge floral stem wire about ½" (13mm) from one end and bend up at an angle. Hook this short end through one of the bucket's side openings that held the original handle; bend the wire again to secure it in place. String 8mm pearl beads onto the length of the wire until there is about 1" (3cm) remaining. Using the pliers, hook and secure the other end of the wire onto the bucket's other side opening.

5 Wrap lace around bucket

Cut a 16½" (42cm) length of 4"-wide (10cm) lace. Wrap the lace around the bucket. Fold the raw edge under and hot glue the lace in place.

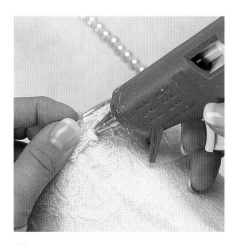

6 Add lace trim along top

Hot glue a length of lace trim around the top rim of the bucket.

7 Add flowers

Hot glue light and dark pink silk roses along the top edge of the bucket.

8 Add ribbon

Run the decorative ribbon around the center of the basket, tying a bow in the front, directly opposite the folded lace. Use scissors to trim the ends of the ribbon as desired.

Note: I embellished the ribbon by turning the ends under about 1" (3cm), then gluing a few pearls along the folded ends.

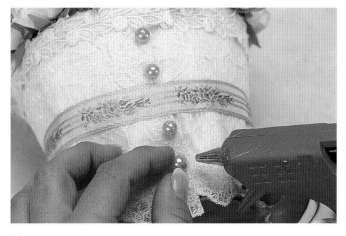

9 Add pearls

Hot glue four pink pearl beads down the back of the bucket, over the folded lace.

TIP I DYED THE PEARL BEADS used in step 9. You can dye white pearl beads simply by submerging them in a fabric dye solution, such as Rit. The longer they are left in the dye, the darker they'll be. White tulle can also be dyed in the same manner.

10 Insert tulle

Insert pink tulle into the basket, fluffing it up a bit. Insert flowers or flower petals into the bucket.

Ring Bearer Pillow

The ring bearer will be even more gallant as he makes his way down the aisle, carrying your wedding rings on this handcrafted pillow. The satin, lace and ribbon cushion and protect the rings beautifully, showcasing the age-old symbols of unending love. Make sure the rings are tied on tightly, then let the little fellow take it away.

MATERIALS AND TOOLS

pencil and heavy paper, for pattern

18" (46cm) ivory bridal satin

white or ivory ribbon:
  ¾ yard (69cm) of 1" (3cm) wide ribbon

  1 yard (91cm) of ½"–¾" (13mm–19mm) wide ribbon

½ yard (46cm) white or ivory lace, 2" (5cm) wide

polyester fiberfill

8mm ivory pearl bead

white or ivory strung-pearl trim

scissors

fabric glue

pins

needle and white or ivory button thread

chopstick or other pointed object

disappearing ink marker

sewing machine

OPTIONAL:

  fabric dye *(tan or ecru)*

  plastic tub, for mixing dye

  towel

1 | Cut out satin squares

Create a square pattern by cutting out an 8½" (22cm) square from a sheet of heavy paper. Fold the ivory bridal satin in half, with the right sides of the fabric on the inside and the wrong sides facing out. Use a disappearing ink marker to trace the pattern onto the fabric. Pin the two layers of satin together in the center of the square, then follow along the marker lines to cut out two 8½" (22cm) satin squares.

2 | Attach ribbon and lace to satin

Cut two 8½" (22cm) lengths of 1"-wide (3cm) white or ivory ribbon and one 8½" (22cm) length of 2"-wide (5cm) white or ivory lace. For an antique look, color the ribbon and/or the lace in tan or ecru dye first. Use fabric glue to attach the two lengths of ribbon to the right side of one satin square, placing them in the center, 1"–2" (3cm–5cm) apart. Glue the lace on top of the ribbon, keeping it centered on the square.

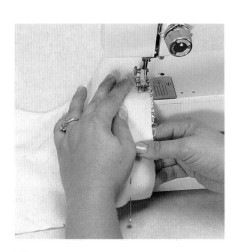

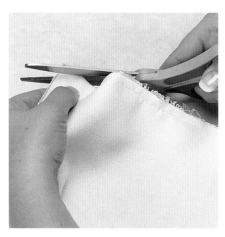

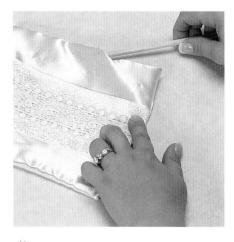

3 | Pin and stitch squares

Place the two satin squares on top of one other, with the right sides of the fabric facing each other. Pin the squares together along each edge. Using a ¼" (6mm) seam allowance, machine stitch around the squares, leaving a 2" (5cm) opening on one side.

4 | Clip corners

After machine stitching the edges, clip each corner of the square in a diagonal cut, as shown.

5 | Turn fabric right side out

Turn the satin squares right side out through the 2" (5cm) opening. Use a chopstick or other pointed object to force out the corners of the square into points.

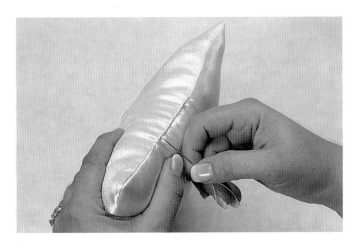

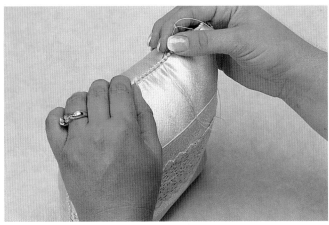

6 Stuff and sew pillow

Stuff the pillow firmly with polyester fiberfill. As you are stuffing, rub the pillow between the palms of your hands to distribute the filling evenly. Hand stitch the 2" (5cm) opening closed using white or ivory button thread.

7 Stitch pearl trim around edge

Hand stitch a length of strung-pearl trim around the edge of the pillow. To do so, first anchor button thread to the pillow, running several stitches through the pillow seam. While you hold the trim in place over the seamline, catch the first pearl with thread. Run the thread through seamline to secure the trim, and continue catching and stitching the trim at every third pearl until you have finished all four edges.

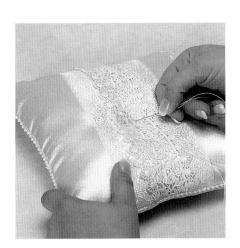

8 Stitch center of pillow

Using button thread and a needle, stitch back and forth through the center of the pillow, passing through all layers of fabric and fiberfill. Pull taut to create a dimple.

9 Add bow to center

Tie the ½"–¾"-wide (13mm–19mm) white or ivory ribbon in a bow. Hot glue the bow to the dimpled center of the pillow. Trim the tails of the bow to the desired length.

10 Add pearl to back of pillow

Hot glue one 8mm ivory pearl bead to the dimpled center on the back of the pillow, as shown. After the glue has set, turn the pillow over. Run one tail of the bow through one ring, and the other tail through the other ring, then tie the two tails in a knot to secure the rings. (Do not tie too tight of a knot, or you may find yourself struggling to release the rings!)

PART 3

Wedding Guest Book
Best Wishes Box
Table Place Settings
Floral Topiary Centerpiece
Wedding Cake Topper
Wedding Cake Serving Set

For the Reception

The wedding ceremony may be the focal point of the wedding day, but the reception is where the real celebration begins! Use the projects in this section to dress up the reception hall so that you can kick off a lifetime of happiness in a truly festive atmosphere. A reception accented with these projects is sure to be the perfect ending to a perfect day.

You'll find instructions for handcrafting everything from a Best Wishes Box for the gift table to Place Settings and Floral Topiary Centerpieces for the guests' tables. If desired, incorporate family heirlooms into your creations to generate a feeling of tradition. After all, part of the fun of developing the décor yourself is using cherished, meaningful items you already have on hand.

Wedding Guest Book

Transform a store-bought guest book into a lovely keepsake by dressing it up and personalizing it with your names. Years after your wedding, you will be able to look at your guest book and remember the family and friends that made your day so special. Choose decorative papers to make a cover so beautiful that you'll cherish the book as much as you cherish the memories!

MATERIALS AND TOOLS

pencil and heavy paper,
for pattern

blank guest book

cream/white decorative paper
(Anna Griffin AG268)

cardstock:

ivory

tan

ivory lace trim (two varieties)

8mm ivory pearl beads

miniature decorative frame

scissors

paintbrush

laminating liquid

fabric glue

permanent adhesive glue

brayer

computer with fancy font,
such as Edwardian, and printer

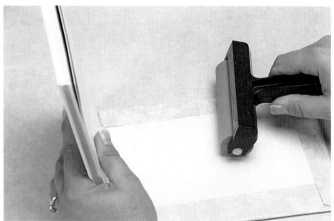

1 Create decorative book covers

Create a pattern for the book cover of a premade guest book, measuring it to fit around the front cover (see *Tip*, below). Trace the pattern onto two sheets of decorative paper, one for the front cover and another for the back cover, and cut each out.

2 Adhere back cover

Brush an even coat of laminating liquid onto the back cover of the guest book. Brush another coat onto the back surface of one of the decorative paper pieces cut in step 1. Adhere the paper to the back cover, folding the tabs over the edges onto the interior of the cover. Burnish the paper onto the exterior and interior surface with a brayer. Allow the laminating liquid to dry completely.

3 Adhere front cover

Repeat step 2 to adhere the other piece of decorative paper to the front cover. Fold the paper over and around the spine, so there are no paper edges showing on the front cover.

TIP I BOUGHT THIS WEDDING GUEST BOOK at a craft store, then made my own pattern for the cover. Because the dimensions of guest books will vary, the pattern needed for this project will vary as well. A basic book cover pattern is typically a rectangle, with one flap on each side (see step 1, above). The dimensions of the front and back covers for this particular book are 8¼" x 6¼" (21cm x 16cm). To make the pattern, I simply traced around the book cover onto a sheet of heavy paper. I then used a ruler and pencil to add four 2"-wide (5cm) tabs, one on every side, to be folded over each edge—top, bottom, side and spine. After cutting out the pattern, I tested and adjusted the size and shape before using it to create the covers.

4 | *Add interior panels*

Cut two sheets of tan cardstock ⅛" (3mm) smaller than the cover dimensions. Adhere the cardstock to the inside of the front and back covers with laminating liquid, burnishing with a brayer to eliminate any air bubbles. Brush 2–3 coats of laminating liquid over the top of the cardstock to seal and secure it. Allow the laminating liquid to dry completely.

5 | *Add lace to covers*

Use fabric glue to adhere two lengths of ivory lace trim—one on top of the other—to the back cover. Place the lace parallel to the binding, about 1" (3cm) from the spine, as shown. Trim the lace along the top and bottom edges of the book. Add two more lengths of ivory lace trim to the front cover, adhering it in the same manner.

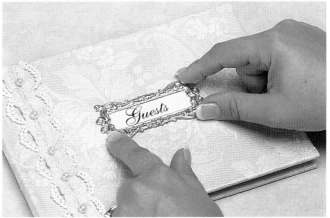

6 | *Add pearls*

Use fabric glue to adhere ivory pearl beads along the length of the lace trim, spacing them evenly.

7 | *Add cover tag*

Use a computer printer to print a "Guest Book" tag in a fancy font, such as Edwardian, on ivory cardstock. Trim the tag to fit inside a miniature decorative frame. Adhere the frame to the tag with permanent adhesive glue, then position the framed tag on the cover as desired. Use permanent adhesive glue to adhere the tag to the cover.

Best Wishes Box

When your wedding guests want to know where to put their gifts and cards, just point them in the direction of this pretty card box. Decorated with flowers, pearls and the newlyweds' monogram, this charming box will accent your wedding gift table beautifully. After your wedding day, you can use this box to hold your cards and photos for years to come.

MATERIALS AND TOOLS

hinged wooden cornice box,
12¾" x 12¾" x 3¼"
(32cm x 32cm x 8cm)

wooden oval plaque,
5" x 7" (13cm x 18cm)

wooden monogram letter,
1½" (4cm) high

pencil and heavy paper,
for pattern

12" x 12" (30cm x 30cm) sheets
of coordinating decorative paper:
    blue floral (Anna Griffin AG147)

    coral floral (Anna Griffin AG 159)

strung-pearl trim

acrylic paint:
    pink

    light teal

paintbrushes

scissors

craft knife

scallop-edged or other
decorative-edged scissors

hot glue gun and glue sticks

permanent adhesive glue

laminating liquid

decorative paper punch
(ribbon-and-bow design)

fine-grit sandpaper

brayer

safety goggles

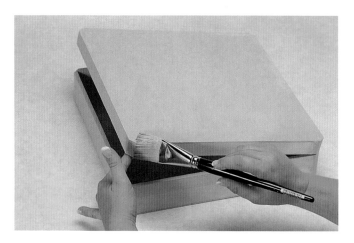

1 Basecoat wooden box

Paint the entire wooden box, inside and out, with pink acrylic paint. Allow the paint to dry completely, then lightly sand the surface with fine-grit sandpaper. Brush on another coat of the same paint, then let the paint dry completely.

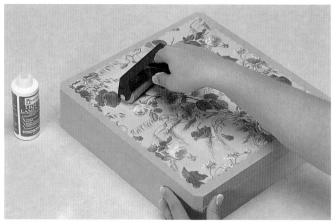

2 Adhere decorative paper to top

Use scallop-edged scissors to trim ¼" (6mm) off each edge of the blue floral decorative paper. Brush an even coat of laminating liquid onto the top surface of the box lid and another coat onto the back of the paper. Center the paper on the top of the box, then burnish it onto the surface with your hand, pressing out any air bubbles. Run a brayer over the paper to further burnish and secure the paper in place. Use a paintbrush to smooth over any laminating liquid that may have seeped out the edges. Allow the liquid to dry completely.

3 Cut out paper panels

Make a panel pattern for the sides of the box, cutting a 9½" x 3" (24cm x 8cm) strip from heavy paper. Round two of the strip's bottom corners, as shown on the panels in the image above. Trace this pattern onto the back of the blue floral decorative paper four times. Cut out each paper panel with scallop-edged scissors.

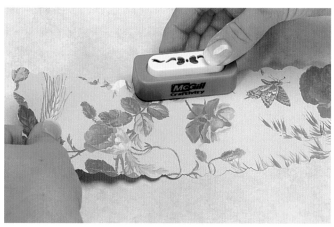

4 Embellish paper panels

Embellish the four side panels with a decorative paper punch, placing the design at the top center of each panel.

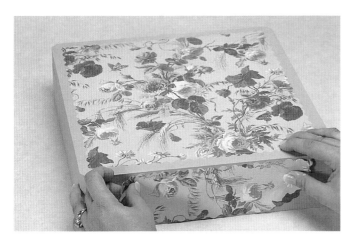

5 | Adhere paper panels to sides of box

Working one side at a time, brush the side surface of the box and the back of the paper panel with laminating liquid. Center the panel on the side, then burnish it onto the surface with your hand, pressing out any air bubbles. Run a brayer over the paper to further burnish and secure the paper in place. Use a paintbrush to smooth over any laminating liquid that may have seeped out the edges. Allow the laminating liquid to dry completely. (This will seal the box lid to the base.)

Note: Be aware that laminating liquid does drip. Be sure to smooth out the drips while they are wet or you'll have to go back and sand them down when they are dry.

6 | Break paper seal

Once the laminating liquid is dry, use a sharp craft knife to break the paper seal along the lid line. Work little by little to carefully cut through the paper, penetrating just a small area at a time. Use safety goggles when you are cutting because, as you apply pressure to the knife, the blade becomes less stable. Continue penetrating the lid line until the blade of the craft knife runs smoothly between the opening. Open the box lid, then sand the edges smooth and touch up with paint where necessary.

Note: Alternatively, you can measure and cut apart the paper panels ahead of time, then glue them on, above and below the lid line, as two separate pieces.

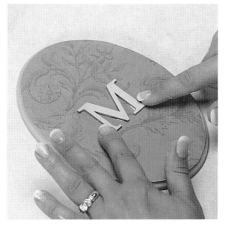

7 | Prepare oval plaque

Basecoat the wooden oval plaque with pink acrylic paint. After the paint has dried completely, sand it and add another coat of paint. Let the paint dry. Cut an oval from coral floral decorative paper to fit on top of the plaque. Brush laminating liquid onto the wooden surface and the back of the decorative paper, then adhere and burnish the paper oval to the plaque.

8 | Add monogram

Paint the wooden monogram letter with light teal acrylic paint. Allow the paint to dry, then adhere the letter onto the center of the oval with permanent adhesive glue. Seal the letter to the plaque surface by brushing over it with laminating liquid. Let the laminating liquid to dry.

9 | Adhere oval to box top

Adhere the oval plaque to the center of the box top with permanent adhesive glue. Arrange the strung-pearl trim along the perimeter of the oval, securing it in place with hot glue.

Table Place Settings

Impress your guests with these fabulous table place settings that include a menu, a name card, a napkin ring and your choice of two favor holders. I combined coordinating paper prints and patterns to create a romantic look. Feel free to select your own colors and decorative paper patterns to complement the style of your wedding. If you like, you can use both favor holders—fill the favor basket with Jordan almonds or chocolates, and fill the paper cone with rose petals to shower on the newlyweds as they make their grand entrance.

MATERIALS AND TOOLS

FOR THE MENU:

decorative paper
(two coordinating patterns)

decorative ribbon
(coordinating with paper patterns)

scissors

decorative-edged scissors

paper glue

self-adhesive foam mounts, such as adhesive dots

hot glue gun and glue sticks

vintage image
(available on Vintage Workshop CD-ROM)

computer and printer

FOR THE PLACE CARD:

decorative paper
(two coordinating patterns)

ivory cardstock

decorative brads

scissors

pin or sharp object

computer with fancy font, such as Edwardian, and printer

FOR THE NAPKIN RING:

wallpaper liner or white cardstock

pink cardstock

decorative brads

pigment ink
  metallic silver

  mauve

scissors

metal ruler

paper embossing tool

decorative paper punch *(square design)*

cosmetic sponge

napkins, to be placed in napkin rings

FOR THE FAVOR BASKET:

peat pot,
2½" (6cm) wide

decorative ribbon

6mm pearl beads

mother-of-pearl buttons, ¾" (19mm) diameter

9" (23cm) length of 20-gauge floral wire

light ivory acrylic paint

paintbrush

scissors

pin or sharp object

craft knife

hot glue gun and glue sticks

needle-nose pliers

ivory paper grass

favors, to fill baskets

FOR THE PAPER CONE FAVOR HOLDER:

pencil and heavy paper, for pattern

pink cardstock

decorative paper

decorative brads

scissors

scallop-edged scissors

paper glue

favors, to fill cones

OPTIONAL:
  disappearing ink marker

Wedding Meal Menu

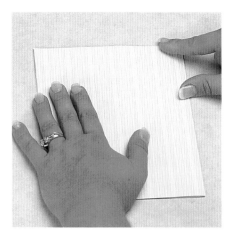

1 Cut paper

Cut a sheet of decorative paper to 7½" x 12" (19cm x 30cm), then fold the paper in half so the decorative pattern is on the outside.

2 Create decorative heart

Find, copy or computer-print a vintage image for the menu cover. (I used a *Vintage Workshop* CD-ROM with copyright-free vintage art.) Use decorative-edged scissors to cut a heart shape around the image.

3 Attach image to card

Use self-adhesive foam mounts to attach the heart-shaped image to the front of the card.

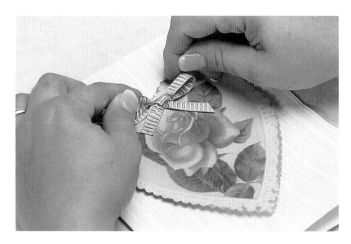

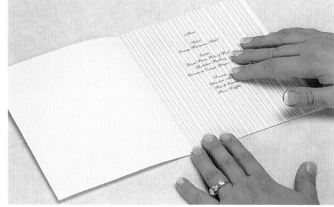

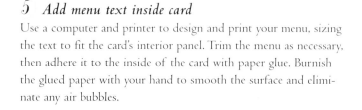

4 Embellish with bow

Cut an 8" (20cm) length of decorative ribbon. Tie the ribbon into a small bow, then hot glue the bow to the top center point of the heart. Trim the ends of the ribbon as desired.

5 Add menu text inside card

Use a computer and printer to design and print your menu, sizing the text to fit the card's interior panel. Trim the menu as necessary, then adhere it to the inside of the card with paper glue. Burnish the glued paper with your hand to smooth the surface and eliminate any air bubbles.

Name Card

1 Cut paper
Cut a 4¾" x 3" (12cm x 8cm) piece of decorative paper. Fold the paper in half, as shown.

2 Print guest's name
Use a computer printer to print your guests' names in a fancy font, such as Edwardian, on ivory cardstock, leaving plenty of space between each name. Trim the names to 2¼" x 1½" (6cm x 4cm) rectangle tags.

3 Attach name to card
Cut a 2¾" x 2" (7cm x 5cm) piece of decorative paper that coordinates with the paper used in step 1. Center a name tag on the 2¾" x 2" (7cm x 5cm) decorative paper, as shown. Attach the two papers to the folded card with a decorative brad. (The brad will go in easier if you create a hole first with a pin or sharp object.)

Napkin Ring

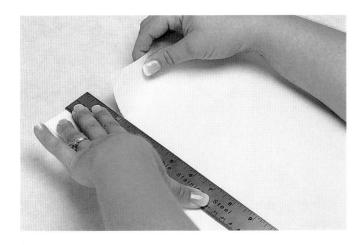 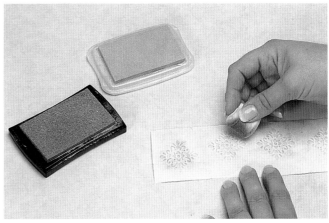

1 Tear paper strip
Tear a 2½" x 9" (6cm x 23cm) strip of wallpaper liner or white cardstock. To tear, hold a metal ruler in place on the paper surface, then pull the paper toward you against the edge of the ruler.

2 Emboss design on paper
Use a paper embossing tool to emboss a design along the entire paper strip. With a cosmetic sponge, apply metallic silver pigment ink over the embossed surface. On top of the silver ink, apply a layer of mauve pigment ink, which should pick up the design of the embossed surface.

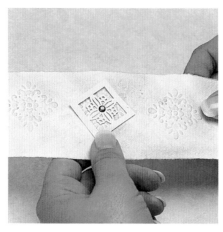

3 Punch out design
Use a decorative paper punch to punch a square design into a sheet of pink cardstock. Trim just outside the edges of the punched design, as shown.

4 Attach design to paper strip
Use a decorative brad to attach the punched-out design to the front center of the embossed paper strip.

5 Roll paper and secure
Roll up the strip, leaving an opening large enough to accommodate a napkin. Secure the end of the strip to the paper it overlaps with a decorative brad, as shown. Roll up a napkin and insert it into the ring.

Favor Basket

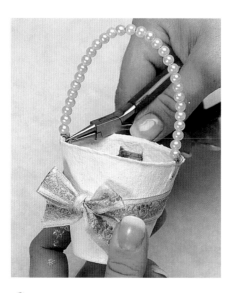

1 Paint and embellish peat pot
Basecoat a peat pot, inside and out, with light ivory acrylic paint. Allow the paint to dry, then use a craft knife to cut two parallel, vertical slits—both large enough to accommodate the decorative ribbon—about ¼" (6mm) from the top edge. Run a length of ribbon through the slits, as shown. Hot glue a mother-of-pearl button directly below the slits.

2 Form handle
Bring both ends of the ribbon around to the front of the pot and tie a bow. Using a pin, poke two holes exactly opposite each other—one to the left of the bow and one to the right—about ¼" (6mm) from the top rim of the pot. Loop and secure one end of the 20-gauge floral wire through one hole. String 6mm pearl beads onto the wire and shape the beaded wire into an arched handle.

3 Finish with grass and favors
Loop and secure the other end of the wire through the remaining hole. Stuff the pot with ivory paper grass, then add wedding favors of your choice.

PAPER CONE PATTERN

Use a photocopier to enlarge this pattern 200%.
Cut out the pattern, then trace it onto a sheet of
heavy paper. Cut the pattern out of the heavy
paper and use it for steps 1–2.

Paper Cone Favor Holders

1 Cut out pink cardstock

Lightly trace the pattern onto a sheet of
pink cardstock with a pencil or disappearing ink marker. Cut along the lines with
scallop-edged scissors.

Note: Most disappearing ink markers work on paper.
However, it is recommended that you first test the
marker on the paper you'll be using.

2 Cut out decorative paper

Trace the pattern onto a sheet of decorative paper with a pencil or disappearing
ink marker. Cut along the lines with
scissors, trimming ¼" (6mm) off each
edge to make the decorative paper slightly
smaller than the cardstock.

3 Complete cone

Center the decorative paper on top of the
cardstock, then use paper glue to adhere
the two pieces together. Place one end of
the paper over the other, rolling it into a
cone. Preserve the cone shape by securing
the paper with a decorative brad, as
shown, then fill the cone with favors.

Floral Topiary Centerpiece

Placed at every table, this floral topiary centerpiece will help create a festive atmosphere for the reception. Incorporate old family candlesticks into the design if you have any, or purchase new ones from home decorating or craft stores. Your creativity and careful attention to detail comes shining through in this marvelous showpiece of paper and silk roses—a sure bet for impressing your guests!

MATERIALS AND TOOLS

8" (20cm) crystal candlestick

foam ball, 5" (13cm) diameter

white or ivory tulle bouquet collar

2½ yards (2.3m) white or ivory sheer decorative ribbon

50 white (or ivory) paper roses, with stems

30 pink (or peach) silk roses, with stems

corsage pins

scissors

hot glue gun and glue sticks

chopstick

fabric stiffening spray

1 Secure bouquet collar to candlestick

Fill the well of the crystal candlestick with hot glue, then insert the handle of the bouquet collar into the well. Firmly press the collar into the well, then allow the glue to set.

2 Insert foam ball and flowers

Rest the foam ball on top of the bouquet collar. Trim the stem of each rose to about 1½" (4cm). Begin inserting the white paper roses and the pink silk roses into the ball, arranging them in a ring around the bottom, where the ball meets the collar.

3 Glue ball to collar

Lift the foam ball and apply hot glue to the surface of the collar. Press the ball onto the collar to secure it in place. Allow the glue to set.

4 Finish adding flowers

Continue to add white paper roses and pink silk roses in rings around the foam ball until the entire surface is covered. As you add the flowers, insert a corsage pin into the center of each blossom. This adds a decorative touch and keeps the flowers in place.

TIP YOU COULD ALSO USE LIVE FLOWERS to create a wonderfully fragrant floral topiary. Follow the same steps, but use a green floral foam ball soaked with water instead of a foam ball.

5 | Add ribbons

Cut several 7" (18cm) lengths of sheer decorative ribbon. Tie one end of each ribbon to the openings on the plastic rim of the bouquet collar. If there are no openings, use hot glue to secure the ends of the ribbon to the collar rim.

6 | Curl ribbons

Curl each ribbon around a chopstick very tightly. While the ribbon is wound around the chopstick, spritz it with fabric stiffening spray. Hold it for a few seconds, then release the ribbon.

7 | Pin collar fabric

If desired, you can perk up the collar around the base of the topiary. To do so, lift the tulle and secure it in place with corsage pins, inserting the pins beneath the ribbon, through the tulle and into the foam ball. Continue pinning the ribbon until you've made your way around the entire base.

{ANOTHER ROMANTIC IDEA}

This monogrammed sash, a lovely accessory to the pink and white topiary, is simple to make and easy to incorporate into your table decorations. To make the sash, cut 2"-wide (5cm) organza ribbon to the desired length. Use a computer printer to print out your monogram letter(s) in a fancy font, such as Edwardian. With a disappearing ink marker, trace over the letter(s) onto each end of the ribbon. Embroider the letters by hand stitching over the ink lines, using two strands of embroidery floss. Fold each side of the end back to form a point; stitch or hot glue the pointed end in place; then finish by stitching a few pearl beads directly beneath the monogram.

Wedding Cake Topper

Tailor the look of your wedding cake by providing your own cake topper. This "love-bird" topper adds a sweet touch to a sweet treat, and it can also become a keepsake. Many couples freeze the top layer of their wedding cake and eat it at their first anniversary celebration. If you follow this tradition, keep the topper as a memento of the day and use it for a second time on your first anniversary!

MATERIALS AND TOOLS

round papier-mâché box,
3" (8cm) diameter

blue floral decorative paper
(Anna Griffin AG 147)

beads:

    4mm crystal bicone beads

    6mm pink crystal bicone beads

    6mm ivory pearl beads

white and pink silk floral picks

white or ivory button
(with center holes),
1½" (4cm) diameter

love-birds embellishment

26-gauge beading wire

light teal acrylic paint

pencil

paintbrush

scissors

laminating liquid

hot glue gun and glue sticks

flush cutters

needle-nose pliers

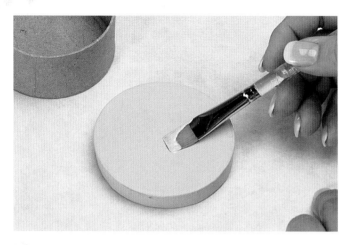

1 Paint box lid

Coat the lid of the papier-mâché box with light teal acrylic paint. Allow the paint to dry completely.

2 Cover box with decorative paper

Measure and cut a 1½" x 9½" (4cm x 24cm) strip of decorative paper to fit around the box. Brush an even coat of laminating liquid onto the papier-mâché surface of the box and another coat onto the back of the paper. Place the paper around the outer surface of the box, burnishing to adhere it and eliminate any air bubbles. If any excess paper hangs below the bottom rim, fold it over the edge and adhere it to the bottom surface. Trace around the base of the box onto a sheet of the same decorative paper. Cut this base panel out and adhere it to the bottom surface with laminating liquid, brushing over any excess liquid that seeps out.

3 Add beaded wire around box

Put the lid on the box, then place the box upside down on your work surface. Cut a 9½" (24cm) length of 26-gauge wire and use needle-nose pliers to make a small loop at one end. String several 6mm pearl beads, 4mm crystal beads and 6mm pink crystal beads onto the wire, then place it around the box, right above the lid line, as shown. Secure the end of the beaded wire by fastening it to the loop, then trim off any leftover wire with flush cutters.

4 Make pearl arch

String 6mm pearl beads onto a 6" (15cm) length of 26-gauge wire, leaving about ½" (13mm) of wire on each end. Bring the two ends of the beaded wire together to form a teardrop-shape, then run both ends through the center holes of a 1½"-diameter (4cm) button. Pull the wire taut, then twist the wire ends together to secure the pearl arch.

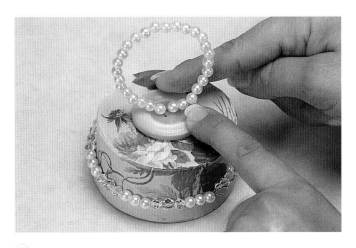

5 *Attach pearl arch to box*

With the box still lid-side down, place the pearl arch on the center of the box surface, as shown. Use hot glue to secure the button to the box.

6 *Add crystal ring*

String eleven 4mm crystal beads onto a 4" (10cm) length of 26-gauge wire, leaving about ½" (13mm) of wire on each end. Bring the two wire ends together to form a ring, then twist the ends together a few times to secure the shape. Slide one 6mm pink crystal bead over the twisted wire. Hang the crystal ring from the pearl arch, securing it by wrapping the wire around the top center of the arch.

7 *Add love birds*

Place the love-birds embellishment under the crystal ring and hot glue them in place on top of the button.

8 *Embellish with flowers*

Hot glue pink and white silk floral picks around the love birds, covering the top of the box.

Note: To create pink floral picks, I dyed some of the white picks with pink fabric dye.

Wedding Cake Serving Set

With these easy projects, you will have an entire cake and champagne set ready to go for your wedding day. Your cake or desserts will look simply gorgeous on the presentation plates, which are dressed up with a few beads. For the wedding cake knife, a bit of embellished ribbon adds an elegant look—and a cake server can be made to match in minutes. The toasting flutes are a finishing touch, made festive with ribbons and flowers. These projects require minimal time, but their impact will be great!

MATERIALS AND TOOLS

FOR THE WEDDING CAKE PRESENTATION PLATE:

glass or porcelain plate with decorative openings along rim

crystal candlestick

beads:
   6mm crystal beads

   4mm pink pearl beads

32-gauge wire

flush cutters

needle-nose pliers

glass glue

FOR THE TIERED DESSERT PLATES:

3 different-sized glass plates

2 crystal candlesticks (can be different sizes)

crystal-beaded fringe

scissors

hot glue gun and glue sticks

glass glue

FOR THE WEDDING CAKE KNIFE:

silver cake knife

white or ivory wired ribbon, 1½" (4cm) wide

5mm pearl beads

scissors

liquid seam sealant (*Fray Check*)

hot glue gun and glue sticks

FOR THE CHAMPAGNE TOASTING FLUTES:

2 toasting flutes

white ribbon

white silk floral picks

scissors

fabric dye (*tan or ecru*)

plastic tub, for mixing dye

towel

Wedding Cake Presentation Plate

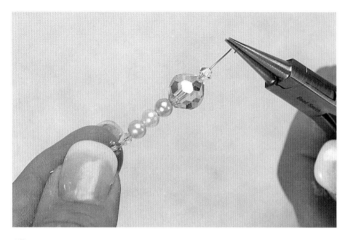

1 Assemble bead dangles

Use flush cutters to cut several 2½" (6cm) lengths of 32-gauge wire. With needle-nose pliers, form a small loop at the end of each wire. Slide crystal and pearl beads onto the lengths, then use the pliers to bend the straight ends of the wire, curving each into the shape of an earring wire.

2 Add foot and hang bead dangles

Add a "foot" to the plate by adhering a crystal candlestick to the bottom of the plate with glass glue. Hang the bead dangles from the openings around the rim of the plate.

Tiered Dessert Plates

2 Add tiers

Add tiers by stacking two more glass plates on top of the fringed plate. To do so, first center a crystal candlestick on top of the fringed plate, followed by a smaller glass plate. Add another crystal candlestick, centering it on the plate, and top it with the smallest plate. For added security and stability, glue the candlesticks to the plates with glass glue.

1 Add fringe to rim

Use hot glue to adhere beaded fringe around the rim of the largest glass dessert plate.

Wedding Cake Knife

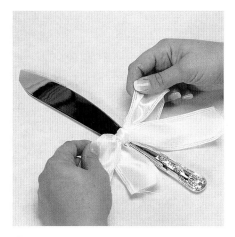

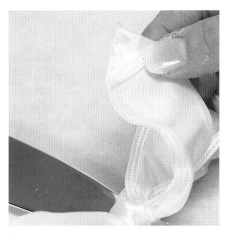

1 *Tie ribbon around knife*
Cut a 26" (66cm) length of white or ivory wired ribbon. Tie the ribbon in a bow around the top of the knife handle.

2 *Create pointed ribbon ends*
If the cut edges of the ribbon fray, trim them and apply liquid seam sealant to prevent further fraying. On each end, fold back both sides of the ribbon to create a point, as shown. Hot glue the folded-back ends to the back of the ribbon.

3 *Embellish ribbon*
Hot glue three pearl beads along each end of the ribbon—one at the center point, and one on either side. If you also have a cake server, give it the same decorative treatment as the knife.

Champagne Toasting Flutes

1 *Dye embellishments*
For a vintage look, dye white silk floral picks and white ribbon in a solution of tan or ecru fabric dye. Dunk the flowers and ribbon in the dye for a couple of seconds, then remove. Lightly pat them dry with a soft towel, then allow the flowers and ribbon to air dry completely. (If desired, the flowers and ribbon can remain white.)

2 *Add embellishments to flutes*
Tie the dyed silk flowers around the base of each flute, twisting the wire stems to secure each flower. Finish by tying the dyed ribbon into a bow directly below the flowers. Trim the ends of the ribbon as desired.

PART 4

Thank You Notes
Memory Album
Wedding Picture Frame
Wedding Memento Box
Honeymoon Book
Keepsake Ornament

For After the Wedding

After the vows have been exchanged, the last bites of cake have been savored and the lazy days of the honeymoon have drawn to a close, the task of preserving memories begins. A bride's work, it seems, is never done. But remember, just because it's "work" doesn't mean you can't enjoy it!

In this section, you will find fun and easy ways to wrap up your wedding experience. Crafted with fabric, paper, ribbons and lace, the Memory Album and Picture Frame provide unique ways to display special photographs. And to keep your wedding and honeymoon memories alive, you'll love the Wedding Memento Box and Honeymoon Book. If you loved giving your wedding a handcrafted touch, you're in luck—these final projects are guaranteed to keep your creative juices flowing!

Thank-You Notes

The thank-you note provides an opportunity to express your gratitude and appreciation for all the kindnesses shown to you on your wedding day. Let the thank you also express your unique style as a couple. This is the final touch of your wedding, and recipients are sure to notice the thought that goes into the note, from the design of the card to the message you include.

MATERIALS AND TOOLS

cardstock
cream

ivory

decorative paper
(in two coordinating patterns)

decorative ribbon
(to match decorative paper),
¼" (6mm) wide

decorative brad

scissors

decorative-edged scissors

pencil

paper glue

hot glue gun and glue sticks

plastic shape template,
decorative rectangle

self-adhesive foam mounts,
such as adhesive dots

computer with fancy font,
such as Edwardian, and printer

1 Cut and fold cardstock

Cut an 8" x 4½" (20cm x 11cm) sheet of cream cardstock. Fold the cardstock in half, as shown.

2 Add decorative paper

Cut an 8" x 4" (20cm x 10cm) sheet of decorative paper, then trim along the edges with decorative-edged scissors. Fold the paper in half and place over the top of the cream cardstock, as shown. Use paper glue to adhere the decorative paper in place.

3 Add decorative paper accent

Cut a 3½" x 3¾" (9cm x 10cm) piece of coordinating decorative paper, then trim along the edges with decorative-edged scissors. Fold the paper in half and place over the folded card, as shown. Use paper glue to adhere the paper in place.

4 Make "Thank You" tag

Use a computer to print "Thank You" in a fancy font, such as Edwardian, on ivory cardstock. Use a template to trace a decorative rectangular design around the text, then cut out the tag. Use a self-adhesive foam mount to adhere the tag to a piece of cream cardstock. Trim the cardstock, leaving a border of ivory around the tag.

5 Attach tag

Place the "Thank You" tag on the front of the card, centering it on the lower half, below the decorative paper accent. Attach the tag with a decorative brad.

6 Add bow

Tie a decorative ribbon in a small bow and trim the ends. Place the bow on the upper half of the card front, centering it above the "Thank You" tag and hot gluing it in place.

It makes sense to decide well ahead of time what kinds of papercraft projects you'll be doing for your wedding. If you give yourself enough time to plan, you can coordinate all your papercrafts and generate your own "line" of wedding stationery. Consider establishing a theme for your wedding crafts. If, for example, you decide on a vintage floral theme, you can introduce it with your invitations and carry it through the entire wedding, right to the final thank-you notes. When creating your own stationery, feel free to mix, match and make variations of any project in this book, such as the napkin holder and the favor box shown here. Your projects will look great and will leave a fabulous impression on your guests. Paper often costs less when you buy larger quantities, so plan to buy all the paper you'll need for the wedding—for invitations, programs, favors, name cards and thank-yous—at the same time.

Memory Album

Preserve your wedding day memories in a custom-made memory album. This particular album has a vintage look, but you can alter the design however you see fit with your choice of decorative paper patterns and embellishments. Collect photographs, cards and other mementos to make memory pages on standard 12" x 12" (30cm x 30cm) sheets of scrapbook paper. These pages can easily be inserted and removed by untying and retying the ribbon along the spine.

MATERIALS AND TOOLS

wooden-cover (or hardcover) memory album, 13" x 13" (33cm x 33cm)

12" x 12" (30cm x 30cm) sheets of coordinating decorative paper:
 blue floral (Anna Griffin AG147)

 coral floral (Anna Griffin AG 159)

1 yard (91 cm) white wired ribbon, 1½" (4cm) wide

lace stickers

miniature decorative frame

light teal acrylic paint

paintbrushes

scissors

laminating liquid

dimensional clear gloss medium

brayer

acrylic matte finish spray

screwdriver

fine-grit sandpaper

computer with fancy font, such as Edwardian, and printer

memory pages, completed

1 | Basecoat book covers

Use a screwdriver to remove the metal screws that hold the album covers together. Basecoat both sides of the wooden album covers with light teal acrylic paint. Allow the paint to dry, then lightly sand the entire surface. Add another coat of paint and let dry.

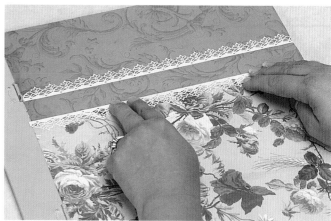

2 | Adhere decorative paper

Trim one sheet of decorative blue floral paper to 9" x 11½" (23cm x 30cm) and one sheet of decorative coral floral paper to 5" x 11½" (13cm x 30cm). Brush an even coat of laminating liquid onto the front cover and another coat onto the back of each piece of paper. Place the papers on the front cover, positioning the blue sheet to cover the lower two-thirds of the surface and the coral sheet to cover the upper third, as shown. Be sure that the edges of the paper are flush with the top, right and bottom edges of the cover. Burnish the paper with the palm of your hand, then use a brayer to further burnish and remove any air bubbles. Brush over any laminating liquid that may have seeped out the edges.

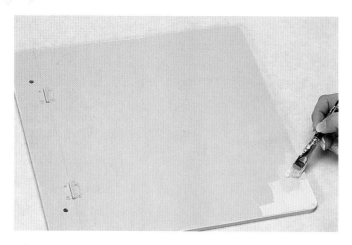

3 | Make cover tag

Use a computer printer to print an "Our Wedding" tag in a fancy font, such as Edwardian, on the coral decorative paper. Place a miniature decorative frame over the text, making sure that the words are centered. Squeeze dimensional gloss medium into the frame, covering the text, until the frame opening is filled, as shown. Allow the gloss finish to set up overnight.

4 | Embellish cover with stickers

Place a lace sticker on the cover, adhering it along the top edge of the blue paper. Add another lace sticker parallel to the first, leaving about 1" (3cm) of space between the two, as shown.

5 Trim corners

Use scissors to trim excess paper hanging over the corners of the book cover.

6 Spray cover

Apply a coat of acrylic matte finish spray over the entire surface of the cover.

7 Add pages and ribbon

Insert your memory pages between the front and back covers, lining up the holes of the pages (which you may need to punch yourself) with the holes on the cover spine. Run the white wired ribbon through the holes on the spine, joining the pages and covers together. Tie a bow at the front center to secure, then trim the ends of the ribbon as desired.

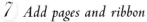

8 Add tag

When the dimensional gloss medium of the "Our Wedding" tag has set, glue the tag to the front cover, between the lace stickers.

Wedding Picture Frame

Don't use just any frame to showcase your favorite wedding portrait—make your own! With its delicate lace and ribbon covering, this frame preserves the timeless romance of your wedding day. To add a personal touch, use leftover lace from your wedding dress or veil. Display your framed picture on a mantle or table, or hang it on the wall to be reminded of your wedding day for years to come.

MATERIALS AND TOOLS

wooden picture frame,
11" x 12½" (28cm x
32cm), with 4½" x 6½"
(11cm x 17cm) window

½ yard (46cm) ivory lace fabric

½ yard (46cm) oatmeal wool felt

3½ yards (3.2m) ivory
or tan decorative ribbon,
1" (3cm) wide

8mm white or ivory pearl beads

corsage pins

light ivory acrylic paint

paintbrushes

scissors

laminating liquid or
adhesive spray

fabric glue

hot glue gun and glue sticks

tape

needle and white or
ivory button thread

fine-grit sandpaper

wedding photograph

cardboard backing for frame

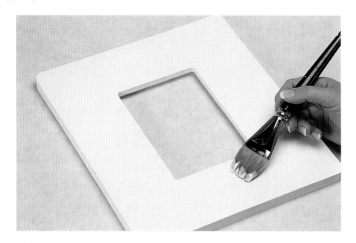

1 Basecoat wooden frame

Basecoat the entire frame, front and back, with light ivory acrylic paint. Allow the paint to dry completely, then lightly sand the entire painted surface. Add another coat of paint. If you can still see the wood grain after the second coat of paint has dried, sand again and add another coat.

2 Adhere lace to front of frame

Brush an even coat of laminating liquid onto the front of the frame, then lay a piece of ivory lace fabric across the surface to cover the frame. (Alternatively, you can apply a coat of spray adhesive to the frame, then press the lace onto the surface.) Wrap the lace neatly around the edges of the frame and adhere to the back of the frame, then trim any excess lace from the back.

Note: If the lace has a scalloped or decorative edge, do not wrap it around the frame. Rather, place one decorative edge right along the top edge of the frame, allowing the scallops to show.

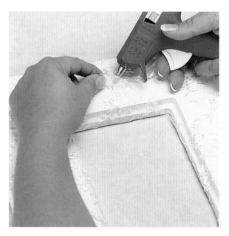

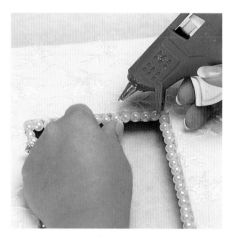

3 Cut lace over frame window

When the laminating liquid has dried, use sharp scissors to cut an "X" in the center of the frame window. Make sure each cut goes right to the corners of the window.

4 Glue lace onto back of frame

Turn the frame over and lay it facedown on a clean work surface. Bring each triangle of lace, created by the "X" cut, around the edge of the window. Adhere the fabric to the back of the frame, using a hot glue gun to secure the lace to the wood surface, as shown.

5 Add pearls

Hot glue 8mm white or ivory pearl beads along the perimeter of the frame window.

6 Make bow

Cut a 12" (30cm) length of white or ivory decorative ribbon. Fold in 3" (8cm) on each side to meet at the center, forming a 6" (15cm) length. Cut a 7" (18cm) length of the same ribbon, then fold in 1¾" (4cm) on each side to form a 3½" (9cm) length. Place the folded 3½" (9cm) length on top of the folded 6" (15cm) length, holding them together in the center. With a needle and button thread, hand stitch through the center to keep the two ribbons attached. Cut a 4" (10cm) length of ribbon, then fashion the "knot" of the bow by wrapping the ribbon around the stitched center and hot gluing it in place.

7 Finish front and insert photo

Cut a length of the same ribbon used in step 6, making it long enough to run across the top part of the frame. Place the ribbon about 1¼" (3cm) from the top edge, then hot glue it in place. Place the bow from step 6 in the center of the ribbon and secure it with hot glue. Insert one corsage pin on either side of the center "knot" for an additional embellishment. Trim your photograph to fit the frame opening, then secure it in the window with cardboard backing and tape.

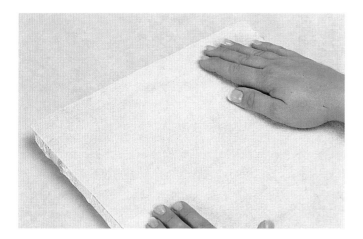

8 Cover back of frame

Cut a piece of oatmeal wool felt to cover the back of the frame. Adhere the felt to the back with fabric glue.

{ ANOTHER ROMANTIC IDEA }

You can take colors, patterns or motifs used in your wedding and incorporate them into the design of the picture frame. This frame includes the decorative paper used to make the wedding invitations on pages 44–47. Any way you design it, you're sure to get a unique look!

Wedding Memento Box

What do you do with all the keepsakes, photographs and mementos from your wedding day? Store them in this special keepsake box, a treasure chest for your most cherished memories. Use stickers and stamps to embellish the box lid with words, sayings and dates that reflect the contents of the box.

MATERIALS AND TOOLS

hinged wooden cornice box,
12¾" x 12¾" x 3¼"
(32cm x 32cm x 8cm)

12" x 12" (30cm x 30cm)
sheets of decorative paper
(in coordinating patterns)

oval paper frame, embossed

transparent text stickers,
love- and wedding-themed

alphabet stickers

miniature decorative frames
(two kinds: round and rectangular)

favorite wedding photograph,
or color copy of photograph

light ivory acrylic paint

metallic gold acrylic paper paint

paintbrushes

brayer

scissors

laminating liquid

paper glue

permanent adhesive glue

acrylic matte finish spray

fine-grit sandpaper

computer and printer
and/or rubber stamps and ink pads

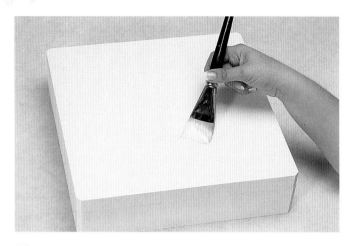

1 Basecoat box

Lightly sand the box. Brush a coat of light ivory acrylic paint onto the entire box, inside and out. Allow the paint to dry completely, then lightly sand the surface of the box again. Add another coat of light ivory paint. Let the paint dry.

2 Adhere paper to box lid

Brush an even coat of laminating liquid onto the top surface of the box lid and another coat onto the back of a 12" x 12" (30cm x 30cm) sheet of decorative paper. Center the paper on the top of the box, then burnish it onto the surface with your hand, pressing out any air bubbles. Run a brayer over the paper to further burnish and secure the paper in place. Use a paintbrush to smooth over any laminating liquid that may have seeped out the edges.

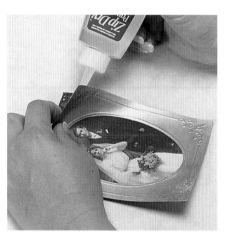

3 Paint oval frame

Brush a layer of gold acrylic paper paint over an oval, embossed paper frame.

4 Glue frame to photo

Select a favorite wedding photo; if you do not want to use the original photo, make a color copy. Place the oval frame over the photo, cropping the image as desired, then adhere the frame in place with paper glue.

5 Assemble framed tags

Using stickers, stamps or a computer printer, add text, such as "Our Wedding," to sheets of decorative paper. Cut the paper to fit inside miniature decorative frames. Adhere the frames to the paper with permanent adhesive glue.

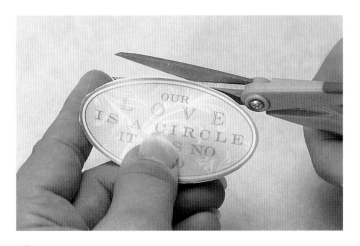

6 | *Make paper embellishments*

Create other paper embellishments using stickers and stamps on decorative paper. You can add transparent text stickers to scraps of decorative paper, then trim around the edges, as shown above.

7 | *Arrange design elements on lid*

Use alphabet stickers to spell out a romantic saying, such as "Forever Love," on the paper-covered box lid. Below the text, arrange the paper embellishments, tags and photo, overlapping as desired for a layered effect. When you are satisfied with the arrangement, adhere all the design elements in place with permanent adhesive glue.

8 | *Add stickers*

If additional components are needed to balance the design, use stickers to add more text, such as the word "Memories," to the box lid.

9 | *Line inside of box*

Brush an even coat of laminating liquid onto the inside of the box lid and another coat onto the back of a 12" x 12" (30cm x 30cm) sheet of decorative paper. Burnish the paper in place with a brayer, then use a paintbrush to smooth over any laminating liquid that may have seeped out the edges. Line the inside of the box base in the same manner.

10 | *Finish with matte spray*

Allow the laminating liquid to dry completely. Apply a coat of acrylic matte finish spray over the entire box, inside and out. If desired, you can sand the edges of the box for an antique look.

Honeymoon Book

The honeymoon is a time to relax and begin your life together as a married couple. After the honeymoon, document your trip in this unique accordion book. Inside, you can keep photographs and souvenirs. You might even add pockets and niches to hold ticket stubs, seashells or other treasures. Feel free to tailor the book to match the theme of your honeymoon destination.

MATERIALS AND TOOLS

blank accordion book, 6½" (17cm) square

12" x 12" (30cm x 30cm) sheets of coordinating decorative paper *(vintage travel theme)*

ivory cardstock

¼ yard (23cm) ribbon, ¼" (6mm) wide

fancy button, ½" (13mm) diameter

large black button, 1½" (4cm) diameter

3 miniature decorative frames *(2 different-sized squares or rectangles and 1 circle)*

scrapbook embellishments, including text stickers and metal corners

decorative brads

paintbrush

scissors

permanent adhesive glue

hot glue gun and glue sticks

laminating liquid

brayer

computer and printer

honeymoon photos and souvenirs

1 Cover front and back panels

Cut two sheets of decorative paper to the same size as the cover panels of the accordion book. Brush an even coat of laminating liquid onto the cover panels and another coat onto the backs of the decorative paper. Place one sheet on each cover, then run a brayer over each cover to burnish and eliminate any air bubbles. Brush a coat of laminating liquid over the paper-covered panels and let dry.

2 Create tag

Use a computer to print "Bon Voyage" or another honeymoon-related phrase on ivory cardstock. Place a miniature decorative frame over the text, then adhere the frame to the paper with permanent adhesive glue. Trim any excess paper along the perimeter of the frame.

3 Add another frame

Adhere a larger frame to a piece of coordinating decorative paper with permanent adhesive glue, then trim any excess paper around the frame. Center the "Bon Voyage" tag within the larger frame, then glue in place.

4 Embellish front cover

Place the framed tag on the upper center of the front cover and glue in place. Add other embellishments, such as text stickers and decorative metal corners, but keep the design simple. Adhere the embellishments with glue, even if they are self-adhesive.

5 Add button

Hot glue a fancy button onto the front cover, centering it along the right edge, as shown. If the button has a shank on the back, be sure to remove it so that the back surface is flat.

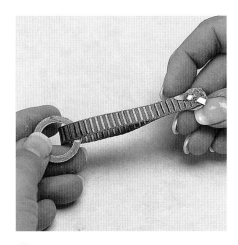

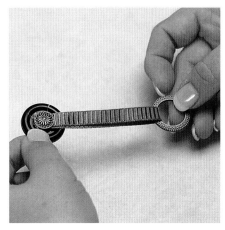

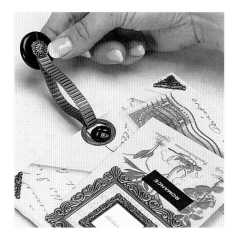

6 Loop ribbon

Cut a 6½" (17cm) length of ¼" (6mm)-wide ribbon. Loop the ribbon through a miniature round frame. Place the two ends of the ribbon together, then insert a decorative brad through the ends, as shown. If the brad tabs are visible from the front of the brad, trim them.

7 Attach button to ribbon

Apply hot glue to the back of the brad, then adhere it to a 1½" (4cm)-wide black button. If the button has a shank on the back, be sure to remove it so that the back surface is flat.

8 Attach clasp to book

Place the frame end of the clasp over the button glued to the front cover.

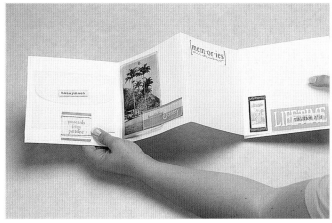

9 Secure clasp

Bring the button end of the clasp around to the back cover, pulling taut. Hot glue the button to the back cover, as shown.

10 Embellish interior pages

Add stickers, scrapbook embellishments, photographs and souvenirs from your honeymoon inside the book.

Keepsake Ornament

Keep the memory of your wedding day alive with this beautiful keepsake ornament. After the wedding is over, save bits of ribbon and lace from your dress, veil, bouquet and gifts. Use the fabric to embellish the ornament, which will serve as a lasting reminder of your special day. You may also wish to make more ornaments as thank-you gifts for members of the wedding party.

MATERIALS AND TOOLS

foam ball, 5" (13cm) diameter

white or ivory computer paper

several lengths of assorted white, ivory and pink ribbons and lace, in varying widths, including 1½" (4cm)

white or ivory ribbon roses

miniature decorative frame (circle)

fabric glue

permanent adhesive glue

hot glue gun and glue sticks

corsage pins

scissors

computer with fancy font, such as Harrington, and computer printer

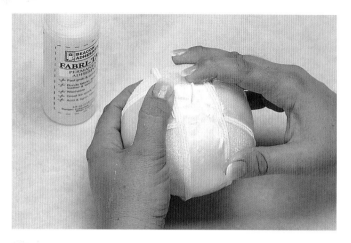

1 Wrap ribbon around ball

Cut two 13" (33cm) lengths of 1½"-wide (4cm) ribbon. Use fabric glue to adhere the ribbon to the foam ball, running the lengths all the way around the ball, perpendicular to each other.

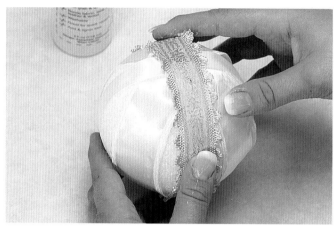

2 Add more ribbon

Continue cutting 13" (33cm) lengths of lace and ribbon and adding them to the ball with fabric glue, as described in step 1. If desired, test the look of the ribbon first by pinning it in place temporarily before gluing it down. If your ribbon isn't long enough, you can cut 6½" (17cm) lengths and run them from top to bottom instead of all the way around the ball.

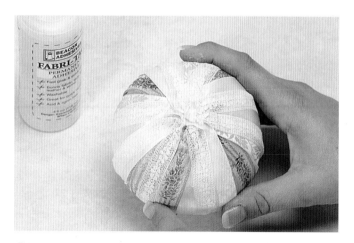

3 Finish adding ribbon

Glue on more lace and ribbon, keeping the design balanced and symmetrical as desired. Continue adding ribbon lengths until you are happy with the look of the ornament. The top of the ornament where the ribbon ends meet does not have to be neat, as this will be covered later.

4 Add hanger

Cut a 10" (25cm) length of ribbon. Create a loop, then pin the ends to the top center of the ball with a corsage pin.

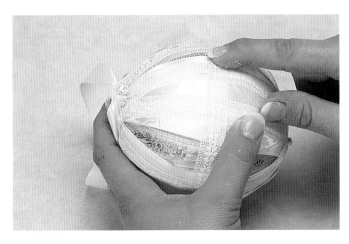

5 Add ribbon across center

Glue on the final piece of lace or ribbon, running it around the center of the ribbon-covered ball, as shown above.

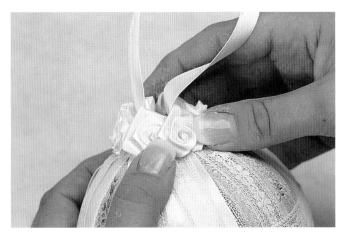

6 Add roses to top

Trim the stems off the ribbon roses. Hot glue the roses to the top of the ball, adding the flowers one by one until they form a ring around the hanger.

7 Add corsage pins

Insert corsage pins around the top, using the pins' pearl heads as decorative elements. Place the pins directly below the ribbon roses.

8 Design and add final embellishment

Use a computer printer to print the names of the bride and groom, the date of the wedding or a favorite saying in a fancy font, such as Harrington, on white or ivory paper. Adhere a miniature decorative frame over the text with a few dabs of permanent adhesive glue. Trim any excess paper along the perimeter of the frame. Position the frame on the center of the ornament, as shown, and secure it in place with a corsage pin on each side.

Note: For added security, hot glue the frame to the ornament before adding the corsage pins.

Resources

Whenever possible, please support your local craft shops by purchasing your tools and supplies from them. Their knowledgeable staff can assist you and answer most any question. Because not every store will have everything you need, I have provided the manufacturer's information for the products that were used in this book.

Anna Griffin, Inc.

733 Lambert Drive, Atlanta, GA 30324
(888) 817-8170
www.annagriffin.com
papers

Beacon Adhesives Inc.

125 MacQuesten Parkway S.,
Mt Verson, NY 10550
(914) 699-3400
www.beaconadhesives.com
general craft glues and adhesives

Delta/Rubber Stampede

2550 Pellissier Place, Whittier, CA 90601
(800) 423-4135
www.deltacrafts.com
acrylic paints and rubber stamps

The Dow Chemical Company

2030 Dow Center, Midland, MI 48674
(989) 636-1000
www.styrofoamcrafts.com
Styrofoam brand products

Fiskars Brands, Inc.

7811 W. Stewart Avenue,
Wausau, WI 54401
(800) 500-4849
www.fiskars.com
decorative-edged scissors, rotary cutters, self-healing mats, personal slide paper trimmers

Hirschberg Schutz and Co.

650 Liberty Avenue, Union, NJ 07083
(800) 543-5442
bridal ribbons, flowers, corsage pins

K&Company

8500 NW River Park Drive,
Parkville, MO 64152
(888) 244-2083
www.kandcompany.com
papers, stickers, frames

Loew-Cornell

563 Chestnut Avenue, Teaneck, NJ 07666
(201) 836-8110
www.loew-cornell.com
paintbrushes

Making Memories

1168 W. 500 N., Centerville, UT 84014
(801) 294-0430
www.makingmemories.com
embellishments

McGill Inc.

131 E. Prairie Street, Marengo, IL 60152
(800) 982-9884
www.mcgillinc.com
paper punches

Me and My Big Ideas

20321 Valencia Circle,
Lake Forest, CA 92630
(949) 583-2065
www.meandmybigideas.com
embellishments, papers

Nunn Design

706 Calhoun Street,
Port Townsend, WA 98368
(360) 379-3557
www.nunndesign.com
small metal frames

Pure Allure

4123 Avenida De La Plata
Oceanside, CA 92056
(760) 966-3650
"Crystal Innovations" Swarovski crystals and jewelry findings

Phoenix Brands

1437 West Morris,
Indianapolis, IN 46221
(866) 794-0800
www.ritdye.com
Rit Dye fabric dye products

Tsukineko, Inc.

17640 NE 65th Street,
Redmond, WA 98052
(425) 883-7733
www.tsukineko.com
ink pads and cleaners

The Vintage Workshop

P.O. Box 30237, Kansas City, MO 64112
(913) 341-5559
www.thevintageworkshop.com
copyright-free images, antique images on CD-ROM

Walnut Hollow Farm, Inc.

1409 State Road 23,
Dodgeville, WI 53533
(800) 950-5101
www.walnuthollow.com
wooden products: frames, keepsake boxes, memory albums

Westrim Crafts

7855 Hayvenhurst Avenue,
Van Nuys, CA 91406
(800) 727-2727
www.westrimcrafts.com
scrapbooking and jewelry-making supplies

Wilton Industries

2240 W. 75th Street,
Woodridge, IL 60517
(800) 794-5866
www.wilton.com
toasting glasses, cake service set